Eastbourne Col
in the Second World War

The years of exile at Radley 1940–45

The Eastbourne Branch in Gonville 1942–45

The HMS *Marlborough* Occupation 1942–46

This book has been researched, compiled and designed by Michael Partridge, David Blake and Simon Wood with assistance from Anthony Robinson, Development Director, Jock Mullard, Publications Manager, and Clare Sargent, archivist, all at Radley.

Published by The Eastbourne College Arnold Embellishers

First published in 2010

ISBN 978-0-9554940-2-4

Published by
The Eastbourne College Arnold Embellishers
Marlborough House
Old Wish Road
Eastbourne
BN21 4JY
UK

Email: ae@eastbourne-college.co.uk
+44 (0)1323 451901

Cover design by Martin Bannon

Printed and bound by
Eastbourne Borough Printing Services
Town Hall
Eastbourne
BN21 4UG

Contents

Introduction

This short publication records in words and pictures the ways in which the College survived the war years 1940–45 and the ways in which these momentous years were celebrated in the years that followed. Most of the content has been published previously and we are indebted to Robert Storrs, Kemeys Bagnall-Oakeley, Philip Mathew (OE), Michael Clark (OE), John Vaughan Wilkes and Charles Wrinch, all sadly deceased, Peter Way and several OEs from the Radley years who took time to record these days for us in words.

OEs of the Radley era (no fewer than 29) have contributed to the project by adding names to photos; they include: Patrick Attenborough, Ken Barton, Geoffrey Bilton, Anthony Churcher, Ian Clayton, Michael Drummond-Brady, Tony Foxley, John Glessing, Philip Gray, Alan Hall, Robin Harrison, Dermot Hoare, Graham Hornby, Richard Horne, Simon Hubbard Ford, John Lock, Brian Luard, Michael Marshall, Peter Milton Thomson, Sir Godfrey Milton Thomson, John Oecken, Ken Ohlson, Trevor Pescud, John Robbins, John Roberts, Peter Townley, John Vinnicombe, Dr Cecil Walkeley and Peter Willoughby.

The photos, most of which are hitherto unpublished, have been placed in the text as near to their context or reference as possible. We would welcome any amendments and additions to the captions.

A Message from the Headmaster

I went to Radley in a very cold January 1978 and remember to this day the then Warden, Dennis Silk, who taught me English in my second year, explaining the plaque that commemorates Eastbourne's evacuation to Radley at the outset of the Second World War. Contemporaries of mine in 'H' Social included AJB Nugee, who was head of house in my first year and Richard Nugee who was in the year above me – both grand nephews of the great John Nugee who took Eastbourne into safety in 1940 and brought it back again in 1945 and, through sheer force of will and hard work, galvanised others around him to re-establish it in the face of austerity and set the foundations for the school it has become today. That the link between the two schools endures to this day is a measure of the welcome Radley extended to Eastbourne and the gratitude Eastbourne still feels. It is also a measure of the numerous coincidences and serendipities that link individuals and families across both schools – from my father-in-law, Michael Pelham Burn, who was in his last year at Radley when the Eastbournians arrived, to that rather lost little boy setting out on a Radley career in 1978 and the now very large man who is the headmaster of the College in 2010.

Simon Davies
Headmaster

The plaque outside Radley Chapel, with words by John Belk

The plaque in the cloisters at Eastbourne

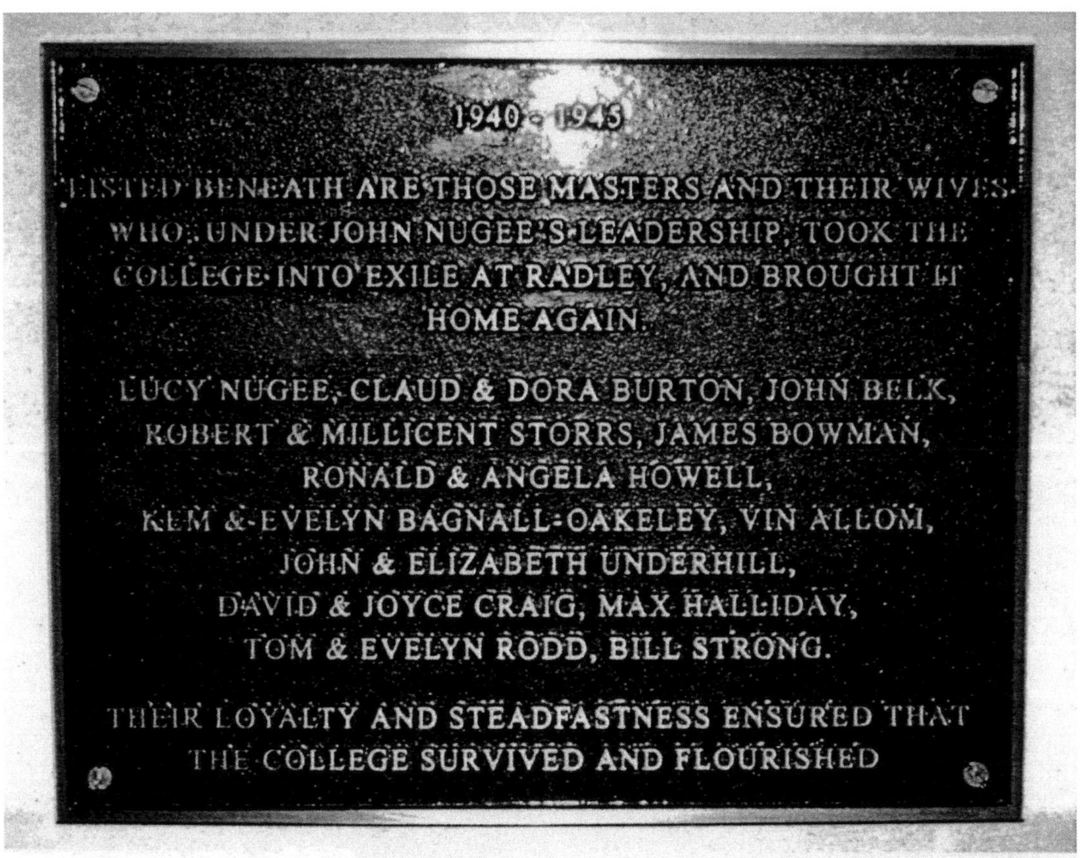

The plaque in the Eastbourne College Chapel, provided by the Arnold Embellishers in 2003

Reunions and Celebrations

Reunions at Radley

The 40th Anniversary

On 27 September 1980 the Committee of the Radleian Society generously invited all OEs who had spent a part of their schooldays at Radley back to a Reunion on OR Day to mark the 40th anniversary of our evacuation to Radley in June 1940. Warden Dennis Silk welcomed OE guests in the Old Gym and 'treated us all to a marvellous half hour of nostalgia, anecdotes and humour'. Peter Sibree replied on behalf of the OEs and presented the Warden with a copy of a book, the first of a number which OEs gave to the Radley library to commemorate the occasion. The day ended with a moving service in Chapel and an informal buffet supper in the Hall.

The 50th Anniversary

Ten years on, on Sunday 10 June 1990, the 50th anniversary of the evacuation, 56 OEs and their wives returned at the invitation of the Warden, Dennis Silk, and the President of the Old Radleian Association, Dr AGS Bailey, to enjoy another memorable day. Following a chapel service and an excellent lunch, Tom Sewell planted an oak tree to commemorate the return and spoke movingly to thank Radley for their wartime hospitality. Following a short concert, Mr Silk charmed Radleians and Eastbournians alike with a delightful address, linking the two

Dr Joe Bailey, President, the Radleian Society; Alan Dowding, Hon Sec Radleian Society; Dennis Silk, Warden; Tom Sewell, College Head Boy 1940

schools through two former Radley masters, John Nugee and Simon Langdale, who became headmasters of the College, and his long friendship with Chris Saunders, our then headmaster, and with Robin Harrison. Highlights of the day included a cricket match between an OE XI (not confined to those who had been at Radley in 1940!) and the Radley Rangers – won convincingly by the visitors. There followed the ceremonial planting of an oak tree, *Quercus Ilex,* by Tom Sewell. The oak and its plaque, and other trees still to be planted in an 'Eastbourne Copse', are the fruits of a fund of over £750 contributed by OEs. The inscription on the commemorative plaque, penned by Tony Henderson, reads *STANT GEMINAE NOBIS INGENTI ROBORE QUERCUS* which, translated, reads 'There stand for us (ie Radley and Eastbourne) twin oaks in mighty strength'.

Dr Joe Bailey, Dennis Silk, Mile Arezina and Tom Sewell plant the tree

The tree as it is today

The plaque by the tree

A commemorative plaque unveiled at Eastbourne

At noon on Sunday 23 June 2002 friends of the College gathered in the Devonshire Wing of the Memorial Building. Headmaster Charlie Bush welcomed the Warden of Radley, Mr Angus McPhail, and all those present, including John Nugee's daughters, Lucy and Tishy, and the junior cricket teams from Radley and the College before their match on College Field. Mr Bush stressed that we were commemorating something that had already been recorded at Radley in a plaque outside their Chapel: the evacuation of the College to Radley from 1940 to 1945. The new plaque records the gratitude that is owed for the leadership of Headmaster Francis John Nugee MC and his staff during the war years, which resulted in the survival and safe return of the College to Eastbourne in 1945. Mr Bush

The panel was unveiled by Headmaster Charlie Bush and Radley Warden Angus McPhail in the presence of the two daughters of John Nugee, Lucy and Tishy

added that cricket and rugby fixtures between the two schools had ceased in the early 1960s, but he hoped that these might be revived in the future. He then introduced Mr McPhail.

Mr McPhail spoke of the very friendly atmosphere that had existed between the two schools during the war years. A Radley boy was even heard to say that the Eastbourne masters were better teachers, whereupon, it was rumoured, the then Warden considered sacking his Science master! On a more serious note, he mentioned that the two schools had managed to maintain their separate identities throughout this difficult period, which was admirable.

The College Chaplain then said prayers for the two schools, after which the Warden unveiled the plaque in the cloisters, which is near to the plaque which records HMS *Marlborough*'s occupation the College buildings during the war. A small bronze plaque has been placed in Chapel by the Arnold Embellishers and this records the names of those members of staff and their wives who served at Radley. Everyone then adjourned to the Long Room in the Howell Pavilion for refreshments, and the cricket match was soon in full swing.

The Radley Lunch, 30 May 2010

The evacuation of the College to Radley 70 years ago was remembered at the lunch held on Sunday 30 May 2010 in honour of those OEs of the wartime generation. The College welcomed nearly 70 guests, including OEs and family members, and the children of members of staff at the time. Speeches were made by Headmaster Simon Davies, Radley evacuee Ken Ohlson (Gonville 1937) and the Development Director of Radley College, Anthony Robinson, who conveyed the best wishes of the Warden of Radley, Angus McPhail. Pictured here is the lunch group on the lawn by the Dining Hall.

Ken Ohlson's Address

Headmaster, Ladies and Gentlemen,

I wonder how many of you remember the '40 Years on' Reunion at Radley? There, after a typically brilliant speech by Dennis Silk, Peter Sibree who, alas, is no longer with us, started by saying 'I have to tell you I hated every minute of it!' It brought the house down.

Personally, I loved our time there and since David Stewart phoned asking me to say something today, I have had a great time recalling those times. You will all have your own memories but here are three of mine – briefly.

Ken Ohlson

First, our contribution to the war effort. We had to man a post on the Oxford to Abingdon road and, dressed in our blue blazers with an LDV (Local Defence Volunteers) arm band, it involved stopping all cars, usually driven by inebriated RAF officers, and checking their identity. We were connected to the Radley cricket pavilion by a field telephone and, one evening, two lads got out to the post without their arm bands. They phoned the pavilion: Major CRB Wrenford ('Jenny Wren') was on duty and they were a little surprised when, very abruptly, he said: 'Right. Hang on.' The Corps was turned out and with 'Pot' Underhill in charge, we were marched past the Warden's House, up a track to the post. Jenny Wren had thought they had said: 'We're held up by an Armed Band.'

Then, perhaps because it's Sunday, a particular service in that lovely Radley chapel. We had a temporary, elderly Chaplain and he began a set of Prayers with 'We will pray for those who go down to the sea in ships and do their business in great waters.' One boy laughed - and it was contagious. John Nugee was not amused and I don't think we saw the Chaplain again.

Finally, the inter-school matches with Radley. They were formidable and I remember one boy, Bobby Darwin, a wonderful cricketer and games player, who put the fear of God into all of us. Sadly, he died very young. They all gave us an inferiority complex until we managed to beat them in a wonderful rugger match – if you've got half an hour I'm sure that Robin Harrison will give you a blow by blow account [see page 47].

So, thank you, Simon, for getting us together again today.

Two weeks ago, kicking and screaming, I was dragged back to my wife's old school for a similar occasion and who should I meet there but an old Blackwater housemaster – Charles Halliday – who went off to be a headmaster elsewhere. He said to me: 'I really loved the College. Everyone there is so welcoming, caring, cheerful and kind.' And that, too, is how I felt about Radley. We had special ties with them during the war with John Nugee and again now with Simon Davies. So, let's drink a toast not only to the College but that the link with Radley may long continue.

Tom Sewell with photos from his album on display in the Dining Hall

Patrick Attenborough, Roger Holloway and Charles Turner, three Eastbourne Branch boys

Anthony Robinson's speech to OEs at Eastbourne College on 30 May 2010

Anthony Robinson, Development Director of Radley College and an Old Radleian himself, brought messages of support and celebration from Angus McPhail, Warden of Radley, who was most disappointed not to be able to attend this 70th anniversary of Eastbourne's arrival at Radley in 1940. Anthony had fond memories of Eastbourne as he had rowed against the College (and lost!) in the final of the National Youth Championships at Henley in 1965 and his grandfather had lived in the Grand Hotel for the last ten years of his life.

He recalled the famous exchange of telegrams between John Nugee and Warden Vaughan Wilkes, recorded in Hibbert's *History of Radley*, when it was proposed and then agreed that Eastbourne should move to Radley. When John Nugee, who had been Sub-Warden of Radley before becoming Headmaster of Eastbourne in 1938, asked if it might be possible to turn up with 300+ pupils, he received the immediate reply: 'Come as soon as you like.' Thus began a very close relationship between the two schools that endures today.

One can hardy begin to imagine the logistical and timetable challenges that faced the combined school. Eastbournians lived in what had previously been Smales Social (H), Wick Hall and Nuneham Park from where they had to punt across the Thames to school each morning. Beds were set up in the new Gymnasium, a disused laboratory, a scout hut and wherever there were flat surfaces. Everyone mucked in. Whatever the stresses and strains, the temporary merger was a triumph of organisation and determination.

Anthony said how thrilled he was to be a small part of the celebrations and how much he looked forward to hearing OEs' stories from those days. He hoped the assembled company would return to Radley in the near future to relive fond memories, visit old haunts and to see how well the Eastbourne Tree had fared in the last twenty years. He thanked everyone for their warm welcome and most generous hospitality.

Radley College in 1944

Warden Wilkes Remembers
From the *Old Eastbournian* of November 1980

Whilst my wife and I were on honeymoon in neutral Ireland in the April of 1940, the Phoney War became real. Norway, Denmark, Holland and Belgium were over-run, France was invaded, and soon the little ships were bringing back from Dunkirk the defeated British army. In early May, after term had begun, I had a telegram from John Nugee asking if Eastbourne could come to Radley. I wired back 'Come as soon as you like' and then telephoned the Chairman of the Council to tell him what I had done. A few days later a special train arrived at Radley station with its weary passengers who had spent most of the previous night in air-raid shelters. Meanwhile we had made what arrangements we could for their accommodation. The Barker Gym (nearly brand-new) could house great numbers – and had shower baths. Most of Radley Vicarage was taken over, beds in the big house at Nuneham Courtenay were provided – the boys ferried daily to and fro across the river – the drawing room of the 'House' (John Nugee never let us call it 'The Mansion' in his day) became a dormitory. School became Eastbourne's dining-room; and soon a new time-table was constructed (by Nigel Fanshaw) to enable both schools to have the use of classrooms and labs.

Perched on the roof of the House we had already constructed a small hut, where dons took it in turn to watch through the night and to report the proximity of hostile aircraft. (When a bomb fell near Abingdon the watchers accurately reported the site where the bomb must have fallen and we were warmly congratulated by the authorities who had immediately been notified.) John Nugee and I watched together once a week, and there concocted a plan for the future – 'What should we do next term?' The plan that emerged was to pool our teaching resources, and make the two schools one unit for teaching, to combine their orchestras and various societies etc., but to remain separate in Chapel and on the playing fields. And that is what we did. The senior forms had 'early school' at 7.30am, while the juniors breakfasted, and so on through the day – the juniors playing games at the end of the morning, the seniors in the afternoons. The plan seemed to work, and to breed a lively and friendly rivalry.

Immense credit must be given to the two Bursars, Charles Jenner and James Bowman, who did a magnificent job in those difficult days of rationing, shortages (of petrol, etc.) and became great friends. The numbers of both schools of course fell by the autumn, with many boys leaving a year or so earlier than normal to join the forces, so that accommodation problems were eased. WR Smale had died in August and his Social building was taken over by Eastbourne, its members distributed among the other seven Socials. We had in the Warden's house three or four Eastbourne boys and their chaplain, Bishop Carey – a glorious man who played the violin to us after supper and to whom our dog became devoted, always accompanying him to Chapel and sitting attentively at his feet. He was succeeded by Charles Neate who of course afterwards became Radley's chaplain and later Sub-Warden.

On Gaudy Day 1940 – celebrated (rather soberly) as usual on St. Peter's day, June 29th – I received a telegram saying 'please cancel instructions to move school to Pitlochry'. I had in fact received no such instructions – but felt grateful to Eastbourne for probably saving us from banishment. Clearly the War Office shrank from banishing two schools, one of them for the second time.

And through those warm star-lit nights of the summer of 1940, Radleians and Eastbournians, masters and boys, prowled about the park, wearing LDV armlets and carrying Boer War carbines (with 10 rounds apiece) with which to repel invaders from the sky. Later, of course, LDV became 'Dad's Army' and we wore uniforms and carried rifles. Meanwhile the telephone exchange was manned nightly by a don (provided with a bed) who, when the alarm came, turned our siren on, and the boys got up and went to air-raid shelters, dug before war began.

Tom Sewell in LDV uniform

Radley and Eastbourne soon settled down to get on with their job; many of the younger masters had left to join the forces (three of Radley's never, alas, to return). Fortunately the staffs remaining fitted neatly – where one school was short of teachers in, say, languages or science, the other was able to fill the gap. But some notable newcomers were enrolled in these years – Raymond King, 'Tonk' Thompson and Paul Crowson, a future Sub-Warden, among them; others came temporarily – a lady historian from Wycombe Abbey (taken over by the RAF), a lady biologist who, a boy told me, was the most savage disciplinarian he had ever met, SPB Mais, of literary fame, a don from Exeter College, Oxford, and a fellow of Trinity College, Dublin – the last a really brilliant teacher and a non-stop talker. Clem Morgan (the Sub-Warden)'s wife and my wife did some teaching too.

Life was busy for the staff – and that was a real blessing because so being, it took our minds off the anxieties and sorrows of those terrible years of war – off the news of deaths of so many boys we had known and loved – three of my first four Senior Prefects among many others. When the war was over and we had a war memorial celebration, the father of one of these (Bishop Eric Hamilton, Dean of Windsor) gave us a deeply moving address in Chapel, and the father of another, General Bernard Paget, unveiled the memorial. And so we carried on, realising, I think, how lucky we were compared with so many of our fellow countrymen at home as well as overseas who were in constant danger, and conscious of the responsibilities which such a privilege must involve – to make the best possible use of our opportunities. But before I end this rambling account of our life in those grim years, let me record one little episode. A bomber from the neighbouring RAF, near Abingdon, returning from a raid had to make a crash landing in a nearby field (the crew happily escaping with only minor injuries). In the next few days a number of fragments of the ruined plane appeared mysteriously in various parts of the College. The CO of the station (with whom I was on friendly terms) rang me to protest (mildly enough) about the thefts, which he (rightly) suspected were our doing, and almost apologetically added that among them was the bandolier of a sentry posted there – would I try to recover it ? I consulted John Nugee and we arranged that our enquiry would not be very searching since we felt that the culprit – whether Radleian or Eastbournian – was a boy who would go far – surely to deprive a sentry on duty of his bandolier was a considerable feat, and he deserved to keep his trophy.

We were not, of course, the only schools to double up for the duration; but I like to think that our 'marriage' was perhaps the happiest of all of them – and that without any doubt the credit for that must go to John Nugee, above all, and to his masters and boys. John Nugee, who knew Radley better than any of us, was so much loved and admired by all of us, Radleians and Eastbournians alike.

JC Vaughan Wilkes

Warden Wilkes was the son of Lewis Vaughan Wilkes and his wife Cicely, who founded St Cyprian's prep school, located where our Memorial Field now stands.

A Radley Don Remembers 1940–45
From *The Radleian* of 1985

Charles Wrinch gives a don's view of the coming of Eastbourne to Radley in 1940. With two intervals, Mr Wrinch taught at Radley from 1928 to 1954. He was Head of English and closely associated with College Drama and the Dons' Plays.

Charles Wrinch

Warden Wilkes, in an unpublished memoir, has vividly related how, after the sudden arrival and make-shift accommodation of Eastbourne College in June 1940, he and the Headmaster, watching together for enemy aircraft in a wooden hut on the roof of the Mansion, evolved the final plan. The outcome, as he noted in *The Radleian* Supplement of June, 1945, was the most successful of all school 'marriages' enforced by the war.

He was, of course, unable to give the principal reason for this success, based as it was on the personalities of the two planners. John Nugee, the only Radleian to have been Senior Prefect for two consecutive years and, surely, after service throughout the 1914–18 war, the most notable of all Sub-Wardens, had – to quote Boyd's History – 'torn himself away from Radley' only two years before to become Headmaster of Eastbourne. John Wilkes had in almost three years embarked on the great adventure which Boyd so acutely and concisely describes. Both were outstanding schoolmasters and, above all, friends. The obstacles facing the Warden were met by tireless energy, magnanimity and the power of a first-class mind. The Headmaster, in his strange predicament, evinced more fully than ever the kindly open-mindedness and strength of a former Sub-Warden from whom junior Radley masters had received such encouragement in the past. Driven out, at short notice, from his new school, he had sought to use Radley as a temporary perch before settling in independently elsewhere, like Westminster and other schools. But having worked out with the Warden a plan for joint harnessing, he gave himself wholly to Eastbourne, keeping the school's ethos and – to quote John Wilkes once more – its 'robust individuality' intact for five years.

John Nugee MC

The two Heads worked in total harmony. John Nugee once remarked that, as the Warden was always amenable to all his requests, he finally felt unable to ask for anything at all.

The hardest problem facing the planners must have been the need for an Eastbourne headquarters, with a home for the Headmaster and his family. It was effectively, if painfully, solved by the temporary suspension of the very distinguished 'H' Social and the re-grouping of its members under other tutors. The house at the head of the Addington Avenue thus became Eastbourne's strategic centre, allowing ample room for the Nugees and also containing RC Storrs' Pennell pupils. The careful allotment of boys from 'H' Social – who were allowed a measure of choice – to other Socials went remarkably well. In 1940 adjustments were always cheerfully accepted.

Immense credit is due to the two Bursars, Charles Jenner and James Bowman. Their relations were no less harmonious than those of the two Heads and their huge problems were never allowed to obtrude on their colleagues.

The essence of the plan was that the schools should become one unit for teaching but otherwise remain separate. We Radley dons found it stimulating and agreeable to be pooled with our Eastbourne opposites, gathering together every mid-morning for direction from the Warden, with the Headmaster at hand to seek desirable enlightenment. Our teaching was, I feel sure, invigorated, and among the boys we found an added sense of competition. The contrasting personalities of Stephen Paton and Maxwell Halliday blended pleasingly on the Modern side. In the Classics HJ Belk was quickly complementary to the Warden and Theodore Cocks. The Science side was strengthened by Eastbourne's Head of Department TE Rodd. RC Burton became a father-figure to us all, well chosen to be Judge in Eastbourne's entertaining Mock Trial. All these, and others to be mentioned below, became our friends and strenuous colleagues, gracefully accepting their changed situation.

Having no exact counterpart in English – unless it were the exhilarating Vincent Allom, whose long service to Eastbourne was lately recognised in a Memorial Service – I vastly enjoyed teaching some outstanding Eastbournians, destined for future distinction. One of these, a prefect, took the liberty of coming down 'after hours' to my home in Lower Radley to read me extracts from a 'period' play which he was writing. He was surprised to be reminded of this when I wrote to congratulate him on his recent knighthood.

Readers of war-time issues of *The Radleian* might often fail to detect the presence of our guests – so separate was each school's identity. *The Eastbournian,* generous to us in its early editorials, reads and looks like a regular home number. Eastbourne 'houses', though somewhat scattered, retained their cohesion. Eastbourne had its own Chapel services and Chaplains, starting with the well known Bishop Walter Carey and ending with Charles Neate, unaware of his Radley destiny. A strong, separate JTC was commanded by JP Underhill, the OE Correspondent, with two housemaster officers RC Storrs and RG Howell. HK Bagnall-Oakeley, living in the house of the College Boatman – engaged in essential war-work elsewhere – organised a remarkably efficient Eastbourne Field Labour Group which won golden opinions in the locality. The school's games, in spite of inevitably falling numbers, were impressively carried on. It was thrilling to see two complete schools watching the annual Rugger match. After the memorable and desirable drawn match of 1941, RG Howell's XVs won two of the remaining three – a fine achievement. On 13th June 1942 Eastbourne celebrated its 75th Anniversary in our midst, playing its annual cricket match versus Lancing (also evacuated) on the same day. It remained unequivocally a school in being.

1941: score 6–6, but Radley scored this try

Some overlapping there was, outside the classroom, to the advantage of all. The direction of the joint end-of-term concerts – one broken up in full swing by the wailing of our siren – was shared by Ronald Dussek and Eastbourne's Dr JH Alden. Air and Sea Cadet forces, unlike the JTC, had officers and personnel from both schools. The numerous Eastbourne societies sometimes invited our dons as guests. For their Shakespeare Society the genial Robin Southam was as natural a Falstaff as for our own. In the unique acted reading of *Hamlet,* the Higher Certificate play, directed by Peter Way, still a boy in the school, and performed by members of the Sixth Form act by act nightly in front of the Mansion, the Eastbournian grandson of the great David Lloyd George was a memorable ghost, uttering hollow adjurations from a real 'cellarage'. I recall most vividly an illustrated talk given to one of our societies by the Eastbourne Art master, Ralph Simpson, from which I learned more about painting than at any time before or since. Equally unforgettable was an address given by the same Ralph Simpson, at the inspired request of the Warden, during an open-air Radley evensong on a summer evening. Soon afterwards he joined the Forces, returning to Eastbourne after the war only to meet a premature death. The school could have suffered no greater loss. How lucky we were to have had him with us.

Eastbournians constantly expressed gratitude to Radley. We, for our part, owed much to them. *Ex Oriente Salus,* their school motto, was extraordinarily apt. If they hadn't come to us, it seems certain that we ourselves would have been evacuated to Pitlochry to make room, like the luckless Malvern, for government use. Eastbourne gave us, in fact, what Boyd's *History* calls our 'greatest stroke of luck during the war'. In addition they gave us the sustaining presence of John Nugee and the resources of his staff. Radley's academic status was higher than at any time, as the record figure of Oxford and Cambridge scholarships, over a wide range of subjects, and the Warden's marvellous production of *The Bacchae* in Greek, all in 1945, clearly reveal.

The large number of OEs coming back to Radley for the 1980 reunion, which I sadly failed to attend, shows how warmly they felt for their temporary home. One of them, who visited me this year, when asked about his experience of evacuation, replied in one word – 'Wonderful'. I know he meant it.

Charles Wrinch

A Radley Boy Remembers
From *The Radleian* of 1985

Peter Way was Senior Prefect in 1941, and a don from 1952 to 1983. He was Head of English and closely associated with Radley's Drama and the Dons' Plays.

Peter Way in 1941

When the Editor of *The Radleian* asked for an article on the arrival of Eastbourne at Radley in 1940 I wondered what could be dredged from the 'dark backward and abysm' of 45 years ago. Authoritative accounts of their five-year exile have already appeared in AK Boyd's history of Radley and VM Allom's of Eastbourne; what little I can provide is drawn from memory and diaries kept at the time. As Eastbourne's first year at Radley was my last before leaving for military service, I can only write of 1940/41. Perhaps others who remember those wartime days (and nights) will be encouraged to contribute their reminiscences of that remarkable time, commemorated in the wall-plaque in cloister, when the two schools lived together under the same roof and were guided by the inspiration and friendship of two great headmasters, JCV Wilkes and FJ Nugee (OR).

College reassembled for the Summer Term on May 3rd 1940, exactly eight months after the outbreak of hostilities; the gestation period of the Phoney War was ending and on May 10th Belgium and Holland were invaded. By June 15th the German army had entered Paris. The evacuation of our South Coast towns under threat of invasion became imperative. On June 18th we were told at Radley to prepare for the arrival of Eastbourne on the 20th for an indefinite stay. Their arrival is described by Allom in Chapters XVII and XVIII of his History:

> We travelled to Radley in a special train, which enabled us both to make the journey without a change and also to take with us in vans all the beds and other

furniture which we were going to need on our arrival. The juniors destined for Nuneham left the train at Culham, one station short of Radley; when the rest dismounted one station further on, it was to find a host of Radley boys and masters there to meet them, who promptly relieved them of their hand luggage, which was taken on ahead. On arrival at the school, the boys were shown to their sleeping quarters and then given a meal in Hall, where they were welcomed by the Warden; and so our five years' exile began.

During the following month at Radley, ninety of the boys slept in the gymnasium, and the rest were divided up into smaller groups who occupied various buildings such as the scout-hut, the cricket pavilion, part of the vicarage, and the deserted wing of a large mansion (Wick Hall) belonging to the local squire. To start with they had no living-rooms, but this situation was soon rectified; the Old Gymnasium (generally used for theatrical performances) and several classrooms were made available, and many of the senior Radley boys who possessed studies invited Eastbourne boys to come and share them; in fact our hosts could hardly have been more hospitable, and our sudden incursion must have made their lives extremely uncomfortable, but they bore it all without a complaint.

It would be comforting to think that the behaviour of the hosts towards their guests was as exemplary as Allom's generous words suggest; what is certain is that the guests were a good deal more uncomfortable than their hosts, particularly during the rest of that first term. But it was hardly a time for any chauvinistic conservatism to express itself, and on Sunday, June 23rd, the spirit of ecumenicism was demonstrated when the Eastbourne chaplain, the charismatic Bishop Carey, preached to both schools in Chapel, his sermon being, my diary observes, 'superb'. And I remember vividly the unusual experience a week later on Sunday June 30th of sitting with our Tutor, 'Tiny' Southam, and other members of the Social (F) on the lawn in front of Lower Market listening to a live BBC broadcast coming from Chapel, only a few yards away, where Eastbourne were singing Evensong.

Term ended on July 29th and with it the first month of Eastbourne's five-year stay, which was to save Radley itself from almost certainly being taken over and sent into exile. The holidays were memorable for a succession of glorious summer days during which the Battle of Britain was fought in skies of unbroken blue. On September 20th the Michaelmas term began; Walter Smale's Social (H) was disbanded, its members distributed among the remaining seven Socials and its building occupied by Eastbourne. The Summer term's temporary arrangements were revised as both schools dug in for the duration. LDV (Local Defence Volunteers, later Home Guard) patrols of dons and senior boys continued to go out nightly to give warning of parachute landings, and air raid warnings increasingly disrupted prep and sleep (e.g. on October 26th: 'The siren wailed at 7.00 pm. We went to trenches and stayed there three hours singing, etc. Came up for some food and at 12.00 am we had an all clear and managed to get to bed.')

Despite these interruptions, life remained remarkably normal, Eastbourne going to the Dons' plays on Friday afternoon, November 1st and Radley the evening of the 2nd, when a number of recently left Old Radleians returned for the annual All Saints gathering. The two schools remained as separate competitive entities for games, and the most stirring moment during that first full term came on November 16th when the 1st XVs met each other. The far touch line of Big Side was lined by Eastbourne supporters in strength and the near by Radley, the cheers of the two schools meeting in midfield at the kick-off and thereafter in a great arch of sound: uniquely, both teams were playing at home.

There were inevitably times when all was not sweetness and light between the two schools: on October 20th, for instance, lunch was 'followed by a harangue on Radley–Eastbourne relations'. The crowded proximity of the two schools, the one preserving its identity in the face of falling members, the other jealously guarding its territory and traditions, could hardly avoid providing an occasional flashpoint. Yet there must have been many quiet influences at work defusing potential trouble, of which the boys were unaware, and we co-existed for the most part in amicable calm.

The Eastbourne school prefects shared Pups' Study with us, and though there were some stresses and strains here too, the statesmanship of their Senior Prefect, KB Mackenzie, friendly, sensible and good-humoured, prevented any serious friction. Some of the best of our generation were to be killed in action within a few months of leaving school, he among them, a great loss for the future.

It was in school periods that some of us came closest to each other, perhaps, sitting together and sharing each others' dons in the classroom and forming friendships in the common pursuit of knowledge. My diary for October 11th, for instance, notes 'the high seriousness of Neighbour and Hale in form': not surprisingly they were to follow distinguished careers, (Professor Sir) John Hale is now a leading Renaissance historian and Oliver Neighbour has recently retired as Music Librarian at the British Library. Gifted dons enriched the lives of both schools and my particular memories are of learning to appreciate Racine from a brilliant teacher, Maxwell Halliday, and of enjoying in divinity lessons the stimulating ideas put to us by Ralph Simpson, the versatile Eastbourne art master who used also to preach and on Sunday, June 23rd, 1941 at Evensong gave 'an extremely good sermon in the form of a parable'. Dr John Alden, the Eastbourne precentor, gave the Sixth forms a weekly period of unison singing and conducted at the joint end of term concert on December 18th, indications of – or perhaps inducements to – growing harmony.

From the classroom came, too, a modern-dress, outdoor production of *Hamlet* in July 1941 in which the charming David Lloyd George, grandson of the great Prime Minister, performed the part of the Ghost, the roof of the Mansion serving as the battlements of Elsinore; he was our only recruit from Eastbourne since they were engaged in their own production, referred to by Allom below. Drama at Eastbourne had ceased under John Nugee's predecessor, but 'One permanent legacy our stay at Radley has left us, and that is the Eastbourne College Dramatic Society.... At Radley we found a school actively devoted to the theatre, and the Headmaster put no barriers in the way of our following suit. The first Eastbourne production was that of comic scenes from Shakespeare's *Twelfth Night* in the summer of 1941, which was produced out of doors at the cottage by Max Halliday, advised for the nonce by Nevill Coghill, who was currently engaged in keeping the OUDS alive during the war. This was followed the next year by a production of Laurence Housman's *Victoria Regina* in the Old Gym, and from that time onwards acting has become a normal part of the school's activities!'

One day perhaps a collection in one volume will be put together of the experiences of boarding schools evacuated during the Second World War: it would make interesting reading. Few, if any, of those shotgun marriages can have worked out as happily as that between Eastbourne and Radley, the first year of whose partnership I was greatly privileged to be a small part of.

Peter Way

Memories of Radley 1940–45

Collected and compiled by Philip Mathew (School House 1942)

Philip Mathew was in School House between 1942 and 1946 and spent most of his schooldays at Radley. After National Service in the RAF, Philip read English at Worcester College, Oxford. In 1954 he joined Monmouth School where he stayed for the next 38 years. He was a much respected housemaster, master in charge of rowing and careers adviser. Through 1989–90 Philip conducted postal interviews with a number of Radley era OEs and staff and this culminated in 1990/91 when the *Old Eastbournian Annual Report* published the outcome of Philip's research into the College's years of exile at Radley, with the reminiscences of Messrs Storrs, Bagnall-Oakeley and several boys. Philip Mathew's work, with the articles that he stimulated, are published on pages 15–44. Philip died in December 2009.

Memories of the Masters

Robert Cyril Storrs, staff 1924–65
Pennell housemaster 1933–53, Eastbourne at Radley 1940–45

Summer holidays 1939 were rudely interrupted by the Declaration of War. This was, of course, not entirely unexpected; many plans had already been made and we had all taken courses in ARP (Air Raid Precautions).

Millicent and I rushed back to Pennell and summoned the staff and other help to get the house ready for the boys' return. Our private day accommodation was in those days all on the ground floor and our dining-room, study and drawing-room were to be the house air-raid shelters. The school carpenters put up pillars and boards to make the ceiling more safe; we all filled bags with earth from the garden – leaving a very nice rock garden – and bagged up all the windows. So that when the boys returned our private living-rooms were completely dark and airless but, we hoped, safer; difficult to live in and fortunately hardly ever used as air-raid shelters. All those enormous windows in the old Pennell had either to be boarded up or covered with thick black curtains. The boys' dining-room was turned into a very efficient curtain factory which enabled us to have the house perfectly blacked-out by the time the boys returned.

Millicent and I cherish one very happy memory of that summer. Max Halliday, who then lived in a perfect flat in Powell House, attended by a very smart and efficient valet-cook, turned up one day in shorts to help fill up our bags, attended by his valet. Max was a very willing but not very efficient bag-filler – but there was a war on and he would do his duty!

The cloister arches and the windows of the north block of the Memorial Building were bagged up in case shelter had to be taken in school time and every window was prepared for air-raids and black-out.

Once the boys returned, we tried to do everything normally but all the rifles were removed from the armoury in case the Germans came over, and our cadet corps, armed with swagger sticks, were the only protection this part of Sussex had from the invading Germans. I remember so well, in the summer term, hearing the gunfire in northern France echoing round the Downs.

Donald Perrens was due to arrive to help with the Physics in September 1939, but I imagine he was a keen member of the Varsity Training Corps and he was called up into the army. I don't think it is generally known that he had a distinguished army career before he joined the RAF and distinguished himself there. This was rather a blow to us, but it seemed to be mitigated by the arrival in Eastbourne of a man – I believe his name was Lane – who claimed he was the senior science master and a member of the OTC in a school in Ramsgate that had evacuated to the west country and that he and his wife had refused to go. He did take some Physics classes and did help with the corps, and he got himself established as secretary to some ARP committee in the Town Hall. Then one Sunday in May he called on Nugee after lunch to tell him that the Town Hall had been told that the Germans had landed in Dover and were making their way across the country. Nugee rang up the Mayor and was told that the Mayor could neither deny nor confirm this, so it seemed obvious it was true. In those days on summer Sundays most of the boys were given a sandwich lunch and disappeared onto the beach, the downs or into the woods until chapel time – 6pm. So it was arranged that our evacuation plans would operate from chapel time. The boys would enter buses instead of chapel and be conveyed to Newton Abbott, where there was an empty school waiting for us – one that had had Richard Butler, formerly of our staff, as headmaster and had recently closed down. An anxious afternoon was spent by all packing up and saying goodbye to our wives and families who were to stay and cope with the domestic staff. Luckily our Bursar thought of ringing up a parent, a doctor in Dover, who assured him that there were no Germans in Dover!

Later, when we did evacuate, Lane refused to come with us and, when we discovered that he had taught no physics and that every practical lesson had been spent on the same experiment repeated each week much to the boys' stupid enjoyment, we realised that Lane had been up to no good. Some weeks later the police came to get more information about him, but we never learnt what he was up to – possibly a fifth-columnist.

This awful experience made us perfect our evacuation procedure, but the school at Newton Abbott was bought by some other school and our Headmaster and Bursar had to travel all over the country to find some other home. This they found at Radley and Nuneham Park and off we all went very soon after.

The evacuation was carefully organised and I think that there is quite a lot about it recorded in the *Eastbournian*.

In early June 1940 our school doctor, Colonel Goodwin, was called up. It so happened that an uncle of mine, Dr Kenneth Storrs, had just retired to a house at Peppard Common near Reading and he was wondering what war service he could do. I asked him to Pennell for a week-end to consider taking Goodwin's place. He had just agreed and was about to go home to make arrangements when we were given 48 hours' notice to quit. So he took our daughter, Fiona, then aged eight months, and her nanny back with him to Peppard, leaving Millicent and me free to wind up Pennell in Eastbourne. (When Fiona was born, just after the war started, our cousins in California begged us to send her to them for the duration of the war. This was a very kind offer, but we have always been thankful we refused.)

When we were evacuated, I was at Radley with the senior school, Millicent at Nuneham with all the juniors, the wives and families, and Dr Kenneth Storrs would call in and deal with any sick at Nuneham, come on after lunch to Radley and deal with the sick there – and bring me news of my wife and daughter!

The day when the school train set off with all the school, hundreds of beds and much luggage for Culham and Radley, Tony Godden and Molly offered Millicent and me a lift in their car. So we were able to tidy things up in Pennell, get our own staff – mostly Welsh girls – off home, before we set off for Berkshire. The journey was interesting and not too easy as all signposts had been removed, together with the names of towns and villages in case these might help invading Germans! However, we got to Nuneham about six o'clock and there Tony, Millicent and Molly found the piles of beds and luggage and settled down reasonably well. I got a lift on, very tired and depressed, to Radley where I was told to go and have a meal in the dining-hall. Imagine my joy when I saw, presiding at the high table, a senior Radley don, one Theo Cocks, who had been a great friend of mine at Westminster. This was wonderful. He fed me, cheered me with a dram of alcohol and took me round to visit my Pennell boys. Ten of them were in an annexe to the vicarage and were being welcomed by the vicar; eight of them were in a disused laboratory in the middle of the school buildings; six were in a scout hut on an island in the Radley lake. All were very tired but well fed and ready to sleep it all off. I dropped into bed, slept well, to be told next morning that there had been a four-hour raid warning which fortunately none of us had heard.

At Radley: Summer 1940

It is very difficult to remember much about what happened to us at Radley for the rest of that summer term. We were all very tired, it was a very hot summer, and the Thames valley was rather different from Eastbourne in hot weather. We had about half the school scattered over a large area of Radley; we had meals at odd times and we taught at very odd times, using the Radley chapel, dining-hall and classrooms when Radley were not using them. I remember arriving after supper some evenings at the laboratories to find them locked up and no-one able to find a key and so conducting classes under the trees outside. This did not matter all that much as we were only revising for the school and higher certificate exams. The boys took the exams under very difficult conditions and I seem to remember that they did very well.

The playing fields were ours while Radley were in school, and we had the Radley boathouse full of boats and a very co-operative Radley boatman called Bint available any morning. I was able to get boys out on a perfect and empty river in eights – rather a change from the windy Cuckmere and our old fours. The Nugees were with the Warden in his lodging and the rest of our staff scattered, but we were honorary members of the Radley high table and well looked after. Those at Nuneham were only a mile away as the crow flies but about 10 miles by road, so contact with the rest of the school was difficult. But they came over for a service in chapel occasionally and some of us were able to get across to Nuneham from time to time.

It was welcome news when we heard that the two school councils had decided we would work together from September onwards.

I cannot over-emphasise the fact that while our staff were really wonderful in making difficult conditions workable and completely unanimous and uncomplaining even when told of the drastic reductions in pay in order to keep the College alive during the war, we were also very lucky in our senior boys. They were wonderful in making the evacuation a success and in keeping things going at Radley.

The First Few Terms at Radley

These were the most difficult for everybody.

As both Radley and Eastbourne had lost quite a number of staff, it was agreed that the two schools should be combined for teaching purposes. This meant that we had too many classes for the Radley classrooms, so the combined schools were divided into a senior and a junior school, each using the classrooms at different times. The senior school started with work before breakfast while the juniors had an early breakfast and then a period while the seniors were eating. Games also had to be at different times and it meant that the two schools never did anything at the same time on a weekday – we were always divided.

Pennell & Powell 1941

Back row: JW Draper, ??, J Strickland, RDG Ingles, BG Luard, HW Underhill, AS Cooper, WD Clayton, AJ Bevan
Second row: JF Holman, DJ Manley?, BS Winkworth, DLS Hodson, J Glessing, ??, ??, ??, JA Churcher, JD Woodhouse, LJM Lawrence
Third row: S Pininski, JA Bennett, JGS Eckersley, RJW Lander?, ??, JN Schofield?, CWH Williams, SR Duncan, N Lea-Cox
Seated: Mr TD Craig, J Harrison, KHL Lamb, J Roadknight, MJ Sawyer, PHC Hamilton, Mr JP Underhill, Mr RC Storrs, Mrs M Storrs & Fiona, PJ Elton, TWA Glenister, PJ Koblenzer, DM Hancock, Matron
Seated on ground: JFM Edwardes-Evans, PMJ Gray, DI Levett, DB Tanqueray, JW Sanders, PH Lyne?, JBW Allan, DM Scrimgeour, GQ Vinson, ABS Tidy, AS Hunt

Teaching, of course, was difficult; there were on a typical day at least twelve periods of school. I don't think anyone ever had to teach all twelve, but one found oneself possibly having an early breakfast and a late lunch and sometimes found it difficult to get into either the early or the late one. On weekdays we had to worship in chapel as a senior and a junior school, but on Sundays we were able to have our own services.

Warden Wilkes was headmaster of both schools and Nugee was really wonderful in the tactful way he was always in the background for support but never interfering with the Warden's authority.

It would be mean to complain about Wilkes, but it would be fair to say that it was not all that easy to work under someone with such a volatile brain. He seemed to love changing things about and as Radley had no system of communication other than a mass of notice-boards in the covered passage, changes were made by little notices on the Warden's board. Such a notice might read: 'As the Warden has a meeting in Oxford tomorrow, today periods X and III will be interchanged' or 'In future Friday's timetable will be exchanged with Tuesday's'. The warden reckoned this kept people on their toes; actually it just irritated them.

Nugee would never interfere. He had been sub-warden at Radley for many years when Wilkes was appointed Warden. His predecessor had been very easy-going and ready to give his sub-warden a free hand and I cannot help feeling Nugee would have found it difficult to serve under the new Warden loyally. For this Eastbourne must be most grateful to Wilkes, as it must have induced John Nugee to seek another job. Often at Radley his staff were a little impatient with Nugee's tact, but looking back on it all, it is also clear that Nugee's quiet diplomacy was one of the main reasons for our five years of peace in war.

One School at Radley

After a few terms, both Radley and Eastbourne numbers fell and some of the younger staff were called up, so it became possible to have one timetable for the combined school. This meant that we all ate, worked and played games at the same time, but we prayed as two separate schools at different times. As far as I can remember, we prayed in the morning and Radley in the evening, and on Sundays we had our own communion service in Radley church.

Our quarters in Radley were odd. One Radley Social – the Radley name for a boarding house – had been given to us as soon as we agreed to live together. The private side was occupied by the Headmaster's family and mine – and we managed to live together for five years and remain friends! The boys' side was occupied by Pennell and the day boys [Powell House], and they filled two large dormitories. They shared the social hall as a prep room, a large room over the war memorial arch, about 100 yards away, as a middle room, and we had about four of the dozen or so studies. The others were occupied by boys from Blackwater, who were scattered over the school buildings, and from Gonville, who had taken over the vicarage – while the vicar retreated into the Radley Lodge – and one or two houses in the village. School House were together in the Mansion and Wargrave in a country house several miles away.

Powell House 1943

Back row: DA Bell, ??, A Churcher, JD Woodhouse, J Rollings, DM Scrimgeour, J Lee, DW Allen
Seated: Matron, J Draper, BG Luard, MS Scrimgeour, Mrs E Underhill & Henry, Mr JP Underhill & Philip, S Pininski, S Cooper, ??
Seated on ground: MJ Brady, AF Toplis

The house we occupied had been Smale's Social, and to make room for us it had been spread round among other Socials and Smale given a small house in the Radley grounds only a few yards away from what was now our home. He obviously resented the Warden's action in taking him out of his Social, but he was polite about it and friendly to us. But it was very uncomfortable for all when he committed suicide during our first term in occupation.

We worked together, each class a mixture of the two schools; the front desks would be occupied by the Radley boys in grey and the back desks by the Eastbourne boys in blue. They never quarelled but seldom mixed, even in practical work in the laboratories.

The laboratory

Radley had recently built a remarkable new building to house all their laboratories with a very large lecture hall at the top. It was made of very thin concrete with enormous windows and was heated by a modern boiler burning powdered coal. The building was quite the coldest in the school, particularly when the special coal was unobtainable – which happened rather frequently as the war and lack of fuel progressed. Radley had spent their all on what was regarded as a wonderful building and were short of apparatus. So we brought the contents of our physics lab up with us to share with them, and we also shared a very remarkable laboratory assistant who had proved absolutely invaluable in Eastbourne and even more so at Radley. Jones, as he was always known, was a clever mechanic and made our apparatus last out the war – and he also kept all our and the Radley clocks and watches in working order.

When lessons were over, we were quite separate schools. To start with, we had our own tables in the Radley dining-hall, but their eating habits were so different from ours that this did not last long. The Radley dons had their High Table and their boys' behaviour below them did not seem to concern them. Our housemasters begged leave to eat with their houses, but this worried the Radley dons and indeed the kitchen staff, because we found their method of serving food rather disorganized. So we persuaded the bursar to provide food for us in a separate hall – the old school hall at the opposite end of the cloisters. It was just large enough for us and was much appreciated. As I had been the principal rebel in the Radley hall, Nugee made me responsible for the feeding in our own hall. We were given a stewardess who supervised the laying up and supply of food, but we had to keep three boys off school to act as servers. They had an old, noisy, stupid trolley rather like the large trolleys on railway platforms. This they loaded with all the crockery and cutlery from the Radley pantries, laid the tables, returned to the kitchens for the hot food and other items, trolleyed them along and put them in the oven. After the meal all had to be returned to the pantries, brought back and re-laid for each meal. It was a hard day's work, but enjoyed as a change by most, and I doubt if it seriously affected their work. Eating together like this – something Eastbourne had never done before – did help the school to maintain its identity.

The two schools never combined for games. Radley kindly allowed us a couple of pitches and a pavilion at the far end of their magnificent playing field and there we played our cricket and football and had our sports. I imagine that we were allowed to use their golf course and rackets courts, but I don't remember any Eastbourne boys doing so.

Rowing was run by each social owning their own boats and the school using about six eights. Almost as many Radley boys rowed as played cricket. I thought we should be allowed the Smale boats, but was disappointed to find they were divided between the other socials, so we were left with none. However, Radley did give us the use of an unwanted boathouse a mile or so downstream and just opposite a lovely little island below Nuneham Park. So each summer a party of us would go into Oxford by bus and call in at Salter's boatyard and pick up a landing-stage, a few fours and a tub-pair, and these we would tow down to our boathouse – an interesting and quite exciting expedition. We brought up our own scullers and oars by furniture van from Eastbourne. There on a really beautiful stretch of the river we enjoyed ourselves, had an occasional race with Abingdon School, a scratch crew from Radley and had our house fours.

Pennell & Powell 1944

Back row: RH McCalman, MJ Brady, GR O'Brien, I MacLennan, RE Needham, WD Clayton
Second row: AF Toplis, DA Bell, JDW Allan, JFM Edwardes-Evans, AD Mitchell, AD Mander, CL Owen, PC Vernon, ABS Tidy, DW de la Hay
Third row; RB Harrison, GA Irwin, ??, DB Tanqueray, JHS Rollings, ??, DI Levett, ??, NB Hill, JW Sanders
Seated: PMJ Gray, AS Hunt, HW Underhill, WD Clayton, Mrs Storrs & Alison, Mr RC Storrs & Fiona, Mr JP Underhill & Henry, Mrs Underhill & Martin, JW Draper, DM Scrimgeour, Matron
Seated on ground: MG Wyles, MP Hamburger, JG Reincke, CS Ward, JJ Congdon, PG Willoughby, ??

We did combine with Radley in the ARP activities, the fire brigade, the LDV etc., but we kept our own OTC and for a time our own ATC. Then it was decided that we should start a Sea Cadet Corps and we joined with Radley for this.

To sort out any difficulties that might arise between two schools living together but in so many ways apart, the Headmaster and the Warden appointed a committee of two Radley and two Eastbourne masters to deal with them. They met regularly but found no work to do. It is remarkable that there just were no real difficulties or troubles.

Evacuees

We were lucky to find such a good home for the school when we had to leave Eastbourne, but we were evacuees. This made little difference to the boys except that they seldom got a chance of seeing the rest of the world or doing any shopping. They were reasonably housed, fed and kept warm. Some thoroughly enjoyed the river and the woods and the spaciousness of the school and its grounds. The tuck shop was open to both schools and was very well run and able to supply some extra food in spite of rationing.

The Eastbourne staff were made members of the Radley common room and were well fed. At first the Radley cellars, so well stocked and enlarged by John Nugee when Sub-Warden, were open to us. But when things became difficult, this privilege was confined to Radley dons and the tuck shop also only served their limited supplies to them. Local shops kept theirs for their old customers and we foreigners had to go short.

I have these interesting recollections: Abingdon was close to enormous cherry orchards at Harwell and in season the shops were full of cherries. I remember going into a shop full of cherries and asking for a pound of them. The shopkeeper looked me up and down and said, 'Where do you buy your vegetables?' 'I am an evacuee and I'm trying to grow my own vegetables with some success.' 'Well, go and grow your own cherries!' We were forced both by their attitude and by our reduced income to be teetotallers, but I was told by a local that if I handed in a black empty bag at an Abingdon baker's shop it would be returned to me with a pint bottle of beer in it. I tried this and was successful for several weeks, but I found it too expensive to continue. That was the only 'black market' I came across.

In those days most of the staff were fairly heavy smokers – most of us pipe smokers; but we just could not, as evacuees, buy tobacco. One day during the Christmas holidays of 1942, Ronald and Angela Howell, John Belk, James Bowman, Millicent and I took the train to Reading which we had been told was full of tobacco. We spent the day visiting every tobacconist and we returned with six ounces of shag between us!

Radley and Eastbourne: The Differences

First from the staff point of view. Until the arrival of John Nugee as headmaster in 1938, the Eastbourne masters very seldom met as a staff. Before the Memorial building was built, there was no common room, only a dungeon under Big School where the bursar's one and only secretary worked and where masters could leave their gowns and hoods. In the new building we were provided with a common room of reasonable dimensions and there we kept our belongings; each had a pigeon hole for messages and cups of coffee were served in the break (previously many of us used to retire to Cave's Café in Terminus Road each break for a get-together over coffee). Meetings were held at the beginning of each term in a classroom to arrange moves etc, but never to discuss policy in education.

This did not mean that the staff did not get to know each other. On the contrary, everyone was very hospitable and we were always being asked into each other's houses for drinks and meals. I doubt if there was ever a more friendly community. So much so that the bachelors, who lived together first in a house, 47 Blackwater Road, and then in the Masters' Lodge, arranged an annual banquet to repay their colleagues for the hospitality received.

The headmaster was always held in great respect and affection, and criticism of the way he ran the school was never heard.

On arrival at Radley, we found a staff calling themselves 'dons' and behaving very like Oxford dons, dining together and meeting daily in the Senior Common Room, and holding a monthly meeting in the Warden's lodgings to hear distinguished educationalists and to discuss education in general. These meetings were a pleasure to us, as we did find ourselves rather out of the world in rural Radley and I well remember in particular two of our guest speakers, CS Lewis and the founder-headmaster of Gordonstoun, Kurt Hahn. But many of us got the impression that the Radley dons were more fond of talking about education than carrying the theories discussed into practice. We were also rather shocked at what seemed disloyalty to the Warden, saying 'yes' to his face and then running him down behind his back.

One particular episode struck me forcibly. A senior Radley boy, a scientist, told his father, an influential member of the Radley council, that the Eastbourne masters taught him well and the Radley masters were useless. I reckon it was because of this that the Warden sacked the senior science master and appointed another – and a rather unsuitable one – from another school. At our daily common-room meeting, he explained his action by saying that the master he had sacked had not co-operated in ARP and other war work. Actually he was within a year or two of retiring and not very fit. At the meeting we were all embarrassed by the behaviour of a number of Radley dons who just turned their backs on the Warden while he was talking and muttered their displeasure.

Pennell House 1945

Back row: ??, J Hubbard, JJ Congdon, RH McCalman, PG Willoughby, RH Foote, RTV Brown, MG Wyles, TR Morgan?
Second row: JG Reincke, CS Ward, GR O'Brien, AD Mander, CL Owen, PC Vernon, AD Mitchell, RE Needham, I MacLennan, IR Clayton
Seated: Matron, ABS Tidy, AS Hunt, Mr RC Storrs, Mrs Millicent Storrs, NB Hill, RB Harrison
Seated on ground: RA Blelloch, AI Gosnell, JH Davison, RD Grey, MJ Harvey, WAK Crockatt, AWR Smith

As for the boys, I don't suppose there was a great deal of difference. At Eastbourne, houses tended to be family circles. Housemasters' and house tutors' quarters tended to be very much mixed up with the boys and of course the boys fed in their houses and it is at meal times that we best got to know each other. At Radley this all seemed very different and the 'socials' as they were called had no family characteristics. Radley boys, on the face of it, were very polite – almost excessively. If a Radley boy arrived late for a lesson, he would stand at the door, bow to the master, and try to give a lengthy explanation of how sorry he was for being late.

An Eastbourne boy would tend to slip in and hope to take his place without being noticed or causing a disturbance.

If we were out in the village, passing Radley boys would take their caps off (in those days all boys wore caps) some yards away and hold them out in front of them as they bowed their way past us. Eastbourne boys would not exactly slink past, but would go by with a touch of the cap and a smile!

There was a dear old member of the Radley domestic staff whose job it was to look after and clean all the College lavatories and to manage the sewage farm. His wife told me that when he heard we were going home to Eastbourne he was completely upset. He told her that in all the thirty years he had worked at Radley hardly any boy or master had taken any notice of him. In the five years of our stay at Radley he had got to know all the Eastbourne staff and the boys had made great friends with him. And it was indeed obvious many of the Radley domestic staff were upset by our departure.

On reading these last few paragraphs it sounds as if I was severely critical of Radley. But really we were all very lucky to be allowed to share those five years with Radley. The two schools were squeezed together for five years. They were peaceful years and we parted very good friends, each school apparently the better for having been together.

Memories of Kemeys Bagnall-Oakeley, staff 1927–64 Crosby Housemaster 1936–42, at Radley June 1940–July 1942

At the time of the evacuation I was housemaster of Crosby (actually New Crosby, the former Ascham St Vincent's). We had been in the house for only two terms and we liked ourselves there. We had our own gymnasium, tennis courts and playing field; the small bore rifle range was on the premises and we were near the Links and the Downs. Upper Carlisle Road did get a bit steep by the time we had walked up it for the fourth time in a day and quite difficult, even dangerous, in snow.

We had been warned at the beginning of the summer term 1940 that we might have to evacuate at short notice and then on Sunday May 26th the headmaster announced that the Germans were at Dover and that we must prepare to evacuate the next day, possibly that night, there being a rumour that the enemy was to attempt a landing at Pevensey. We spent a hectic afternoon packing up; my wife sent our nannie and children by taxi to her brother in Surrey and I arranged for a farmer friend to take my hens. In the middle of this flap a boy (John Turner Ettlinger, Pennell 1939) arrived with six pheasant chicks in his respirator case and we put them under a broody hen. It was a welcome interlude; it was a long time before the farmer realized what they were. Meanwhile James Bowman telephoned to a parent in Dover who, a bit grumpy at being disturbed from forty winks after Sunday lunch, assured him that he had not seen any Germans. The plan was called off at about 5pm but no-one told Crosby; it was not until our conspicuous absence from Evensong in Chapel was noticed that we were informed.

On Thursday June 20th it was the real thing; we had been given 45 hours' notice, thanks to there being an OE at the Home Office (Gwilym Lloyd-George). Our previous practice paid off handsomely; we knew what to do. I shall never forget the long train of beds which we ran down the hill on their casters and along Compton Place Road to Seven Gables where they were to be stored.

Beds and mattresses (Pictures Tom Sewell)

We had a special train from Eastbourne station with as many luggage vans as coaches but even so additional furniture vans by road were needed. They could not have petrol for such a long journey and so they ran on Producer Gas, generated on trailers. Air was sucked through burning anthracite in a tall drum at such a rate that carbon monoxide (rather than CO_2) was produced; this gas was then substituted for petrol vapour. Progress was slow as the engines were not tuned for this fuel but the vans got there. The drivers were intrigued at having to fill up at coal yards rather than at petrol stations.

It was a noisy journey with boys rushing about shouting and blowing bugles, very trying for the older passengers, but what upset me most of all was that someone slashed the tyres of my motor cycle; I could never think what I had done to deserve that. I had to push the machine from the station to the college, almost the last straw for me and, not having the right tools under the circumstances, it was a long time before I got it going again.

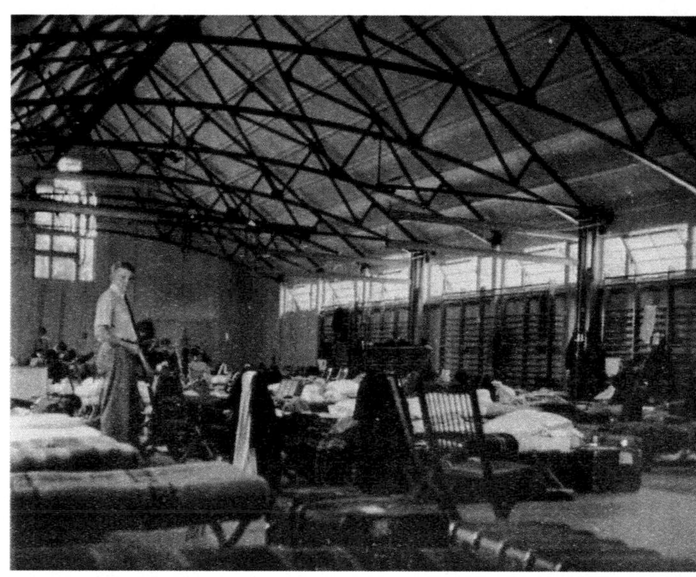

Beds in the Gym (Picture Tom Sewell)

To begin with I was in charge of 104 boys on camp beds in the Gym.

At least I had a room of my own, the PT instructor's changing room, but it was a worrying time; the building had a glass roof and so we had to turn out for green warning without waiting for the red.

Crosby had three day rooms; the Senior Study as we called it, was in the tower and we made it our headquarters; we assembled there in the evenings for house prayers, pocket money and gossip; the cricket pavilion was the Middle Room; it was draughty but it had an open fireplace and a changing room underneath with showers. There was no path to it and so we had to trudge across the grass, possibly in wet weather, perhaps in bedroom shoes. The Prep Room was the most remarkable; it was the museum, in the attic above the armoury. It had no ceiling, just tiles, and on certain winds the rain came in; once I remember a couple of inches of powder snow on the desks. In good weather we laughed at ourselves; the desks were in the bays between the cases; there would be a stuffed badger, a boy, a baboon, another boy, then a mandrell and so on. This room was abandoned as our numbers fell.

The two schools were amalgamated for lessons but we reclaimed our identity for chapel, games and meals. The boys were divided into two groups, laterally as it were, the third and fourth years and the fifth and sixth so that the timetable could be worked on the Box and Cox principle. While one group was in school the other was doing prep, having a meal or playing games. Each boy would have up to six periods a day but the staff who taught in both groups might have ten. They could not teach all twelve or they would get no meals. I had ten periods on one day a week and on another I had seven on the trot but with any luck there were equally long spells of free time. The composers of the timetable were most considerate in that they gave the long spells to those of us who lived out and the 'in one, out one' to the residents. In chemistry, my subject, the Radley boys were following the Phys-Chem syllabus whereas Eastbourne took the two subjects separately. Radley were fascinated to see experiments performed which they had only read about and some of them joined in the practical work with enthusiasm. I found their attitude very rewarding.

The original plan for the evacuation had been for the first and second years to go to Newton Abbot where Richard Butler, formerly housemaster of Gonville, was headmaster but when John Nugee tried to warn him that we were coming it transpired that they too had gone away. In the end we went to Nuneham House, on the other side of the Thames, the stately home of Lord Harcourt. We had been told at Eastbourne that we could not take pets or nannies whereas Winston Churchill had encouraged evacuees to keep their pets, they were so good for morale. My wife arrived at Nuneham with Nannie and two dogs prepared to take rooms in the village if she was turned away, but in fact she was received with open arms by Lady Harcourt who also had two dachshunds (relatives of ours, it turned out) and who envied us our old-style nannie.

Nuneham House

There being no prefects at Nuneham, supervision was in the hands of masters and matrons. I was asked to spend one night a week over there; it made a change for them and enabled me to see my family and the New Crosby new boys of whom there were many, the new house being so much bigger than the old. What's more I escaped from the gym for a night! I would take prep and prayers and go round the dormitories and then descend to the kitchen for dinner with my friend the Crosby chef.

Crossing the Thames was quite an operation, especially after heavy rain upstream. There was a punt on each side; we crossed in one, took the second in tow and brought it back, then went over again in the first. I remember an occasion when some Canadians got loose in the park and shot up the deer; I was asked to bring one back to supplement out rations at Radley. I caused quite a sensation arriving with it across the tank of my motorcycle.

After the summer holidays we were more comfortably housed, the numbers having gone down. I was allotted a little bungalow on the marshland by the Thames. It was obviously meant for summer weekends only but we made a home of it for nearly two years. As I lived out I lost my housemaster's perks of free board and lodging but my wife made ends meet, and enjoyed doing so, with her goats and chickens and ducks; it was just the place for ducks! The whole area was scheduled for flooding in case of heavy rain, to save towns lower down; it became a vast lake with our bungalow apparently adrift in it. The causeway was five or six inches underwater and quite difficult to follow after dark; cycle lamps were limited to a beam only one inch wide and so we had to tack from side to side to see the reeds in the dykes on either side and so keep on the track. Evelyn's feet dipped into the water as she pedalled; it was not the thing to go shopping in 'wellies' in those days. I was still expected to function as a housemaster although I was one and a half miles away and not on the telephone. (Vin Allom was further but he had his boys with him.)

Punting on the Thames
(Picture Tom Sewell)

When I was at school in the First War it was considered unpatriotic to play games. Not so in the Second; parents in the forces obviously preferred their sons to have as normal a schooling as possible. Each game did however try to do one day's work a week out of doors on farms, woods, orchards, maintaining hedgerows, perhaps pulling up fences and each house had an allotment. Unfortunately an Eastbourne boy was caught stealing eggs and that ended the farm work though our seniors continued with some surveying such as calculating the area of irregularly shaped fields; this was to enable the farmers to claim grants. We were flattered that the powers that be accepted our findings.

Their (Radley) telephone system was a comprehensive internal affair but it was connected to the outside world by just one line and only in the day time; there was no night operator. In war time that was not good enough, especially when an Observer Corps Post was set up on the tower. The staff were therefore recruited to man the exchange at night. One's turn came round only once every three weeks and so one never got good at it. On one of my early stints the Warden's wife had a baby and I had to summon the midwife and inform the relatives; her father was CA Alington, formerly Headmaster of Eton but then Bishop (I believe) of Durham. Thank heaven the baby arrived safely!

Another of the operator's duties was to receive the Air Raid warnings. We had a camp bed in the exchange and could sound the siren without getting out of it. I remember thinking of all those hundreds of people turning out to the shelters while I stayed in bed to wait to sound the All Clear.

After six terms the number of boys at Radley had gone down but the number in Eastbourne with no school to go to had risen. The Council were therefore asked to restart an Eastbourne branch of the College. I was chosen to do this, assisted by Vincent Allom and David Craig. Officially I was the Master-in-Charge at Eastbourne; the Puppet Headmaster to my friends. I have written a description of this phase of our history for the College Archives. [see page 53]

Memories of some boys

Hector CB Mackenzie (School House 1935)

It may not be irrelevant to include a note about going there. So far as I remember, it was all done at something like 36 to 48 hours' notice. The Home Office said we must go immediately because invasion was expected, so we went.

John Nugee, our HM, was not long away from Radley so was able very quickly to locate somewhere to go. No easy problem for Radley to accommodate some 320 boys, the staff and house domestic staffs (larger in those days), all at a moment's notice. All credit to the Warden (whose name now escapes me) for an immediate and whole hearted affirmative.

I was a senior prefect in School House when the word came. I was working out my time after the December Cambridge exams; with no intention of going up if I could get into the services. That was none too easy for an 18 year old volunteer because all three services were inundated with the admission and training of vast numbers of new and slightly older conscripts.

My recollection is of returning for breakfast, after all night on the Downs with an LDV patrol, to hear the news. LDV was the predecessor of the Home Guard. One of the first units in Eastbourne was formed by Senior Corps NCOs and masters. We were on patrol the evening after the Secretary of State for War (Anthony Eden?) had called on the radio for LDV volunteers. Arguably, therefore, Eastbourne College fielded one of the first LDV patrols in the land. It had seemed exciting as we set out but less fun up there on the Downs when realization dawned that should – as half expected – parachutists land, we, with a First World War Lee Enfield, a bayonet and five rounds each, would become England's first line of defence!

By mid-morning the following day, we had to be packed up and ready to move to the station. It was not just a matter of seeing to our own property. All the house domestic equipment, Corps and sports equipment was to be packed up to go. The teaching staff, domestic and ground staffs and not least the boys all worked like beavers. That itself could not have sufficed to achieve readiness on time, which was done. Some genius must have planned our activities with extraordinary logistical ability and to my shame I have no memory of who was involved. I have a strong suspicion that the loveable James Bowman, my maths teacher and Bursar, played a major part. At the same time as planning the pack-up, the genius or genii were presumably working away on the telephone making plans for the reverse operation at the Radley end.

The evacuation train (Picture Tom Sewell)

After a last breakfast in houses, all the gear was packed into trunks and we, armed with overnight bags and a packed lunch each, headed for Eastbourne station. On the platform on the south side of the station the longest train I had ever seen awaited us, headed appropriately by a School's class locomotive. It was no matter of stowing gear and jumping in anywhere; embarkation and loading was all pre-planned. All the College and its gear were embarked appropriately to their various destinations at the other end (Juniors out at Culham station, Seniors at Radley). That it all went without visible hitch seems to me to demonstrate that teachers and railway staff in those days have nothing to learn from today's in matter of organization. The 'Eastbourne College Special' followed the obvious route – Redhill, Reading – transferring on to GWR tracks from Southern – Didcot, Culham, Radley.

Radley too were organized to meet us and show us to our 'lodgings'. In School House and quite a few other houses, third year and upwards were put into Radley's vast gymnasium which looked like an army field hospital with row upon row of beds. Other houses' seniors were lodged in other buildings that Radley had released or commandeered in the village. The teaching staff were similarly dotted around. All the juniors were taken across the river with a large share of house domestic staff to the stately home of Nuneham House. By dexterous adjustments of both schools' timetables, it was possible for each school to find classroom facilities to continue the teaching of the individual forms in each school with their own teachers. (I understand that later on the school amalgamated classes and teaching.) This timetable also allowed each school to dine separately in Radley's Hall, assisted by their own domestic staffs. Likewise, we worshipped separately in Radley's chapel. Advantages of the new life were that the seniors of the various houses, cohabiting the gymnasium, came to know each other far better than could have been the case in separated houses at Eastbourne. We also made good friends of quite a few Radleian acquaintances we had made when playing against them for a year or two in the XV or XI. On the other hand, we felt short of contact with housemaster and house tutor, in contrast to feeling that we saw too much of them in Eastbourne!

For me, there was only half a term to go and my form master, being also the Bursar, had many preoccupations besides teaching. By mutual agreement we saw John Nugee with the suggestion that one or two other sixth formers and myself might be found useful war supporting tasks out of school to fill our time. My first was as gardener, or rather gardener's help, at the Cottage (Ferry cottage?) which had been requisitioned beyond the station for John and Mrs Lucy Nugee. 'Dig for Victory' – i.e. grow your own fruit and veg – was all the rage, so I laboured happily with some late (it was June) digging, sowing and planting. Happy work it was; Mrs Nugee was a charming supervisor and conversationalist. Unable to work herself, paralysed early in life by polio, she provided the expert knowledge and with her unique charm and cheerful courage kept up the occasionally flagging morale of the gardener!

Next, with Alex Crookshank (Pennell 1935) and Ian 'Hank' Holloway (Pennell 1936), I cycled daily to a concrete works outside Abingdon. Here, provided with sledge-hammers, we had to break up rejected concrete casts to recover their valuable steel reinforcements. Very hard work it was but it 'cemented' a real friendship between the three of us all from different houses. A bonus was our lunch-hour; authority had turned a blind eye to us (all over 18) taking lunch at a local Abingdon pub.

My only permanent reward for all this work was an inscribed (by Lucy Nugee) and much treasured copy of *Reynard the Fox*. The friendship with Alex and Hank did not survive the war, both of them losing their lives. A great annoyance was that sledgehammers find places to make blisters which oars do not, considerably inconveniencing a rower.

Compared with Eastbourne, Radley's sports facilities seemed quite amazing. A nine-hole golf course (no use to me!), squash courts and a rackets court whereas we had only had Rugby fives. No getting coxed fours round the serpentine Cuckmere bends; here we rowed eights on a stretch of river the best crews in the land were happy to train on. No one has a field of quite the character of College Field but at Eastbourne all but the few who performed there had to go a mile or so to their playing field. At Radley it was all on site.

Liberty in one's spare time was a contrast from Eastbourne. There, only a favoured few seniors were allowed bicycles. One could not walk eastwards of South Street. At Radley, we could cycle into Oxford or where we wished. Curiously, Radley were not allowed personal radios, so we had to hand ours in.

We continued LDV patrols at night, being required to run a checkpoint stopping all traffic on the Oxford to Abingdon road. Those familiar with today's A34 should not get the wrong picture; at that stage of war there was much less than one car a minute at night. We had to wear LDV arm bands on our Corps uniform, drawn by the NCO in charge as we drew our weapons in the armoury. One evening I forgot them, got my patrol to fall in and marched the two miles to the scene of operation. Well after dark I remembered the omission so used the field telephone to the fussy little master who was CO of the Corps [Major Wrenford] and on duty at the College. I was surprised that instead of ticking me off he replied 'Right, I'll come out there immediately.' Half an hour or more later, I heard nearby rustling in the grass; someone stalking me? Eventually there was a loud whisper 'Hst! Is that you Mackenzie? Where are the enemy?' 'What enemy, sir? Have you got our arm bands?' 'You blithering idiot, I thought you said you were under attack by an armed band and I have stalked all the way out here!'

Major Wrenford

The facility to cycle into Oxford enabled me to go to the local recruitment office to volunteer for after term end. I wanted to get into the Royal Navy but was told that the only branch taking volunteers (they were inundated with conscripts) was the Fleet Air Arm who were short of observers, so that became my destiny. So term ended and we took leave of many old and new friends, all wondering what the years ahead had in store. Two years later, back in this country from a first commission at sea, I heard from my younger brother (captain of the Eastbourne XV at Radley) that they were short of players for an OE side. I persuaded my pilot to fly me up to the nearest airfield we could find to Radley. He decided to give the College a good 'beat up', in the course of which half my navigating tools flew overboard. The nearest airfield we found was the now celebrated Greenham Common, then a USAAF base. I think we were the first operational biplane they had seen. They had lots of Saturday transport to Oxford so agreed to run via Radley for me. I gave my pilot a course for home and left him to it.

Walking across to the pavilion to change for the match, a diminutive Radleian approached. 'Were you in the Albatross which flew over this morning, Sir? Did you perhaps drop these by mistake?' He proffered my dividers saying they'd landed right beside him. Grateful for their return, I withheld pointing out that had they hit him, they would have gone straight through his head!

Inevitably as refugees we had a feeling of being the 'poor relations' at Radley during my half term there. This was emphasised by their undeniably superior facilities all round. What made it bearable – no, enjoyable – was the friendliness of all Radleians and staff and their total avoidance of acting the 'rich relations'.

George AA Johanson (Crosby 1935)

I was, in fact, in the Sanatorium at the time of the move so missed all the fun! When I was released, Eastbourne was like a ghost town and I walked up to my house. It was wide open and totally deserted, and then I realised I had no money! By the back door there were a number of empty bottles. I collected these and took them to an off-licence where I got just enough money for the bus fare to my parents' home. When I got up to Radley, I told my housemaster what I had done. He stopped it out of my pocket money!

Roger Sylvester (Wargrave 1936)

We were great diarists in those days. You may get the feel of what it was like to be a rather young and rather earnest schoolboy, a bit wet behind the ears but nevertheless cutting his teeth on the administrative problems we were then faced with.

I know only a little of what happened to the Wargrave boys I was with. OW (Tim) Neighbour (Wargrave 1937) became Keeper of Printed Music at the British Museum. Dick Date (Wargrave 1936) became a headmaster. Sam Maccoy (Wargrave 1937) had a gallant war in the Merchant Navy, returning to sea after some frightening experiences only to be drowned at a very young age. I see his brother, John Maccoy (Wargrave 1935), my closest childhood friend, is now running the Arnold Embellishers...

Wargrave House 1940

Back row: MF Tollitt, PD Burdett, WA Lawson, PGL Townley, PW Palmer, GM Wickman, SE Sylvester, ??
Second row: HLG Sunley, JWPB McIntosh, BC Brodribb, CH Verity, HC Parsons, JB Sylvester, JP Davis, P Warbrick, BC Maccoy
Seated: Miss Hall, RM Date, RD Sylvester, Mr VM Allom, Mr CRB Wrenford, JBC Evelegh, OW Neighbour, Mrs Allom
Seated on ground: DED Foster, JR Turner-Ettlinger, ES Overy, RJM Roberts, RH Walker, AJS Watson

Wick Hall with its lovely tree-lined avenue is now sadly not what it was. I met a Radley boy working on a fish farm near Oban who tells me there are still Dockar-Drysdales around. The old walled garden is a housing estate and the lawn on which we played innumerable games of croquet against the D-Drysdale daughters (in crinoline-like skirts) is also a part of that development. If I close my eyes I can smell the hay fields across which we used to make our way to the Thames. On the tow-path Tim was cornered by the Radley VIII and ducked. I crouched in the bushes watching and shivering. It was not all quite so harmonious as correspondence in *The Radleian* would suggest...

It amuses me to think that less than three years later I was performing much the same administrative functions for a parachute brigade in Burma. The College gave me a good grounding. Nugee asked me to return as Head of School in the place of Tom Sewell (Crosby 1935) but I was too busy learning Hindustani and driving lorries in the London Blitz for the offer to be attractive. I expect it was stupid of me. It was certainly very generous of him. I like to think that many of the things that have happened to me since can be traced back to that short episode of 'Radley'. Ralph Simpson valiantly tried to teach me to paint in the grounds of Nuneham Courtenay, the site of Auburn, loveliest village of the plain. Though neither it nor he was successful, I now run a small art gallery in the Highlands. Ralph encapsulates for me the extraordinary dedication of a very gifted staff who made the best of what was then on offer...Allom gave me the run of Oxford in my free time which is why I finished up six years later at Balliol and can pole a punt from the right end.

Diary of the Evacuation of Wargrave House from Eastbourne

Monday 17th June
6pm Was called to Allom's study. He said that the College was to evacuate on Thursday but I was to tell no one. I was to organise the evacuation of the House since we had no house tutor.

8–11.30pm Prepared a rough timetable for Tuesday and Wednesday. Evelegh (Wargrave 1936) helped with the lists of boys to do various jobs.

Tuesday 18th June
6.30am Wrote out organisation before breakfast. Given leave off morning work. Saw the Matron, Miss Hall and Allom about things needed from the town.

11am Brought 1,000 labels and string. Searched shops for cord and eventually purchased six balls from Timothy White's. Arranged with Mackenzie, the photographer, for house photo at 2pm. Continued lists until 12.30pm.

12 noon. The College told of the evacuation in Big School. After lunch briefed prefects about their jobs: Tim Neighbour with six boys removed the books from the House Reading Room to Pennell. They were carried in blankets.

Evelegh and his party dismantled the desks in classrooms 14 and 15 and carried them over to Powell House.

Date (Wargrave 1936) was in charge of a party that took sheets, bedding, etc, down to Big School. Warbrick (Wargrave 1937) and Lawson (Wargrave 1938) strung labels.

4pm Allom gave me tea.

In the evening everybody brought their books up from College and decided which they should take with them and which should come on later by lorry. These were tied up and taken either to Pennell or to the New Buildings.

7.30pm Packing.

11.30pm Finished notices setting out organisation for Wednesday.

Wednesday 19th June
6.30am Evelegh and Parsons (Wargrave 1937) left to load the lorries.

7am Studies stripped. Miss Hall helped with the washing up. After breakfast all the beds were dismantled and taken round to Pennell. The system was to piece one bed together in the road and put two more on top of it, then wheel the whole lot round. Date and his party dismantled the common-room.

11am Lemonade and biscuits. Tuck-boxes packed. All the luggage was piled outside and chalked. The middle-room strung 900 labels. Cycled down to town with Evelegh to buy Miss Hall leaving presents. We both chose brooches.

4pm Took disorganised games in the Wargrave back garden. Overy (Wargrave 1940) was tossed in a sheet which split when we tried to do the same thing to Evelegh. Date climbed onto the roof from the cubes and jumped into a sheet.

Reading hour. The prefects had their last game of Blindman's Bowman. (A species of leap-frog played in socks, named for some reason after the College Bursar.) The teams were: Date, Evelegh, Roberts, Sylvester R, vs Verity, Parsons, Overy, Sylvester J.

6.30pm Last Evening Chapel.

7.30pm Allom and Mrs Allom gave me dinner. Drank burgundy for the first time.

9pm House Prayers. Allom made a speech about the future of the House and we all sang 'Auld Lang Syne'.

Thursday 20th June
After breakfast everybody gathered on the front path with their belongings in suitcases, rucksacks and bandoliers made from blankets. Miss Hall and the maids waved us off from the gate.

At the station Wargrave filled three compartments. The train left at 11am. We wondered when we would see Eastbourne again. I was in a carriage with my brother John, Tim Neighbour, Sam Maccoy and Allom. After Reading the train passed Wellington, Allom's old school. At a station near Nuneham the juniors got out. At 3.15pm we arrived at Radley where the Wargrave party collected on the platform. We were conducted by a Radley boy to a pony and cart which stood outside the station. The nine of us crammed our belongings in and were soon on top and underway. It was a bright sunny afternoon; we must have been a curious sight.

We got to Wick Hall at about 4pm. Mrs Dockar-Drysdale came out and showed me round the rooms. Some beds and a few mattresses had been provided but the rooms had not been used for years. All the pink plastered walls were crumbling and there was nowhere for us to put our clothes, shoes, etc. The only washing facilities were one basin. We had a ground-floor living-room with oak panelling from an old Oxford college chapel that had been rebuilt. All round the walls were family pictures of the Dockar-Drysdales. The room looked out onto a fine lawn.

Wick Hall

5pm Tea up at the College, some distance away. Then we arranged our books in the living-room and I wrote more lists until 10pm by the light of a candle.

Beautiful summer's night. We slept until 6.30am next morning.

Jenniss Paine (Pennell 1937)

I was 17 in June 1940 and in Pennell House. Robert Storrs was housemaster and Phillip Wyatt house tutor. I shared a twin study, near the gas rings, with John H Ellis (Pennell 1936); we were both working for the civil service exam, for entry to the services, which was to be held in Brighton in July.

We were all aware that the war was going badly; just how badly was brought home to senior boys when we had to do several 'patrols' on the front near the Martello Tower at night, under RSM Strong. I do not remember being issued with ammunition; we would have been a great deterrent! It was a very hot summer and soon we could hear the gunfire and see the flashes in the night sky. The evacuation, when it came, happened very quickly, I think within a week. The HM announced in Big School that we were going to Radley and Mr Storrs told JHE and me that he had rung our parents and we could go home until we sat our exams and then rejoin the College at Radley, as best we could. The College left by special train; I also left by train, to Maidstone, Kent, across country taking about six hours!

Eastbourne College Corps of Drums 1942

Back row: BEN Lyte, HW Underhill, GE Martin, AW Goodinge, MF Tollit, WJP Decie, S Pininski, RDG Ingles, WD Clayton, G Binns

Seated: JA Bennett, RAE Wilson, TWA Glenister, N Lea-Cox, DLS Hodson, WB Sams, IDM Mackenzie

Seated on ground: BG Luard, DB Tanqueray, DM Scrimgeour, PO Venn

At the end of the month, I cycled to Buxted to stay with JHE; we caught the train to Brighton every day to sit our exams, which I think were held at the Ship Hotel. With so many distractions, we had neither of us done any revision for weeks and were in poor mental shape! With exams finished, JHE and I set off to cycle to Radley. It was still very hot and we did the journey in two days, sleeping the night on the Bisley rifle range. Radley on our arrival bore no resemblance to a conventional school; it must have been a nightmare for the staff of both schools. Pennell older boys were camped in the Radley scout hut which was some distance from the main buildings. I do not remember doing any work, but do remember blowing a bugle from the top of the tower to signal the end of periods, as it was forbidden to ring the school bell.

While the rest of the school sat their normal school certificate exams, Alex Crookshank (Pennell 1935), JHE and I were given war work, for pay, at an iron foundry in Abingdon, where we spent carefree days straightening iron rods with big hammers. At night we did

Home Guard patrols and guard duty at the main gate. At the end of term, I cycled home through London. John and Alec were both killed in the war and I did not see them again. My exam results were predictably bad, but my father suggested I sit the exam again in March 1941. On return to Radley, I found the school numbers more than halved, and most of the senior boys had left. Pennell and Gonville had taken over one of the Radley 'socials'; we were all relieved to find Mr and Mrs Storrs in residence; there was some permanence after all! Mr and Mrs Howell had a house on the Abingdon road, near the church. KB Mackenzie (School House 1936) was Head of School and Ian Holloway (Pennell 1936), Head of Pennell. Ian and I became good friends with our opposites in Gonville, Peter de Havilland (Gonville 1937) and Harry Newton (Gonville 1937). It was very hard to get used to the odd working hours. We had a period before breakfast and sport or JTC for the rest of the morning, followed by the remaining periods in the afternoon and evening. I personally was taught by unknown Radley masters which also took getting used to, but both schools seemed to function almost normally. The JTC became very relevant. I was CSM of B Company and had to walk down to Mr Howell's house the evening before parade to plan the many excellent exercises we held in the country round the school. The College bugle and drum band had maintained its numbers well, and we played at recruiting drives in both Abingdon and Oxford.

The biggest single difference we found from our Eastbourne houses was the food. We did not like either the food or communal feeding! The Home Guard functioned all through the winter and there were several parachute scares. I do not think the winter was as cold as Eastbourne and there was no snow.

We played rugby against RAF Abingdon and several Oxford colleges, but I do not remember playing Radley. We had little to do with the Radley boys and I do not remember any by name. Modified athletics were held in the Lent term on improvised tracks.

I re-sat the civil service exam in March in Oxford and left Radley/Eastbourne in April. Later that month I played for the College in the seven-a-side competition at Richmond, staying with Harry Newton near the ground. This was my last link with the College and we did quite well. I never saw my friends again; Ian was killed flying and I believe Peter and Harry were both killed in the army. I joined the navy in May. It seems I chose the right service.

Kenneth Ohlson (Gonville 1937)

I was at the College 1937–41 and am now a Governor… I have so many memories of our time at Radley:

Our horror at the thought of having to sleep on the floor during our last night at Eastbourne!

The great welcome from the Radleians; some lent us bikes to cycle over to see the junior boys.

A brilliant day-boy pianist (Rollason) who played the tunes of the day by ear in the Old Gym for hours on end.

A no doubt delightful Chaplain (Gilfillan – he had a son at Radley) who reduced Chapel to hysterics by 'and now we will pray for those who go down to the sea in ships and do their business in the great waters.' An adaptation of Psalm 107, I think. He only lasted about a term.

Our first away school cricket match was against Lancing on the Worcester County Ground. Richard Burton (son of RC Burton, Blackwater housemaster) opened the bowling and may I mention that I got 50! The real highlight was when we were met on return at Radley station by Peter de Havilland (Gonville 1937), who I think was Head of School, with Radley's horse-drawn flat laundry cart, and driven back to the school.

The sadness when we returned after one holiday to find that Mr Smale, whose house we had taken over, had committed suicide.

Catching moles with Ronnie Dowden (Gonville 1940) (now Deputy Lieutenant for Devon) and selling the pelts.

Spending money at a bakery on the Abingdon Road – we cycled there – and eating the jam tarts etc in Mr Neale's (the chaplain) room, listening to music and discussing religion.

The hilarious moment when two small boys on night duty stopping cars on the Oxford to Abingdon road found that they had forgotten their LDV arm bands. They got through on the field telephone to the cricket pavilion where a master (Mr Wrenford, I think) was on duty. He thought they said 'We are held up by an armed band' and all hell was let loose. I believe this was written up in *Punch*.

The formidable Radley cricket side and their lovely coach – Percy Mills – who kept both XIs entranced for hours with cricket stories.

Most important of all: the wonderful caring, enthusiastic way in which Beefy Howell held the whole school, not just Gonville, together. His leadership and drive, not to mention the way in which he prepared us for military service, was quite remarkable. Indeed all the Eastbourne masters did their stuff: I suspect Radley provided the buildings and we the teachers.

George G Brown (Gonville 1938)

I entered Gonville in 1938 and although the war began in 1939, by the summer of 1940 there had been little fighting on the western front and in Eastbourne an atmosphere of tranquility reigned. The summer of 1940 was fine and hot and a magnificent band of the Royal Tank Regiment played light martial airs as, wearing our straw boaters, we used to walk along the front and listen to the band.

Suddenly one Sunday morning we heard a distant rumble from across the Channel – the sound of gunfire – and the front was full of exhausted soldiers, the heels of their boots being worn down to the soles – Belgian soldiers who had been in the retreat. The band continued to play, but the world had changed.

Providentially the weather continued fine and the sea calm and from all along the south coast a flotilla of small boats put out to cross the Channel and assist the Royal Navy in evacuating the Army from the beaches of Dunkirk. A special service was held in chapel to pray for the success of the operation and the last hymn was 'Abide with me'; seldom can the words 'The darkness deepens, Lord with me abide' have had greater significance, or been sung with greater feeling.

About this time my younger brother arrived at Gonville in the middle of term. His sudden arrival was caused by the disintegration of his preparatory school at Seaford. Bowden House had been a preparatory school for over a hundred years, but in the invasion scare they evacuated to a large house in the West Country, walked in a crocodile up to the front drive, a master knocked on the front door, and to their dismay they found another school had arrived there first; that was the end of Bowden House.

In a matter of a few days after these dramatic events, a special train evacuated the College, which then numbered about three hundred and fifty boys, from Eastbourne, and as we departed the bugles of the OTC sounded a fanfare; but whether it was the 'Last Post' or 'Reveille', I do not recall.

When we arrived at Radley there was insufficient accommodation for the whole school and the junior school went to a fine old country house, Nuneham House, on the other side of the Thames. Gonville lived in the vicarage just outside the gates of Radley, but in the daytime we had a common room over the War Memorial Arch.

Whereas at Eastbourne we had eaten in our house dining rooms, at Radley we ate together in a large dining hall. Moreover, while at Eastbourne we had domestic servants to make our beds and wait at table, during the war it was 'self-help', and some of the kitchen duties came as a shock to most of us. Many of the staff of both schools went to the war and for classes the two schools amalgamated. Sport remained in separate schools and some of the early rugger matches generated exceptional spirit and feeling.

Gonville House 1942

Back row: ??, AE Broad, MH Pope, ??, ??, ??, GEH Wilson, RN Horne,??, ??
Second row: IP McNaught, AC Morrison, ??, ??, DW Allen, NS Despicht, ??, ??, ??, JB Alliban
Seated: GG Brown, Matron, AD McNaught, AF Mellows, Mr RG Howell, AB Curtis, Mrs A Howell, DC Liell, RAE Wilson, JBW Goodwin, PAL Scott
Seated on ground: JA Hebditch, Robert Howell, JN Horne

The OTC played a prominent part in those days and it was not long before the Home Guard was formed and boys over seventeen were expected to serve in it. German glider-borne assaults on the Radley College playing fields were confidently awaited. At night no lights could be shown and all windows had to be blacked out.

Whereas at Eastbourne part of the town and shops had always been in bounds to the boys, at Radley the nearest shops were some miles away in Oxford, and these needed a long bicycle ride to reach. Thus the immediate feeling after the move was of a loss of independence and of being cut off from the outside world.

The College debating society continued as usual and although there were never any air raids in the vicinity of the school, by the winter of 1941 the German bombers would pass over almost nightly on the way to bomb Coventry and the Midlands. One night Lloyd-George, the grandson of the Prime Minister, stopped in the middle of his speech: 'You do not believe me?' he said. He looked at his watch. 'In precisely thirty seconds the Air Raid sirens will go to prove me right.' There was silence, everyone thought he was mad. Then the eerie wail of the sirens began exactly as he had forecast. He had noticed that the German bombers were flying over to the Midlands at exactly the same time each night.

As the war progressed, the numbers in both schools diminished and the junior school joined the senior in Radley itself. Some of the Radley 'socials' were taken over by the College and life settled to a comparatively comfortable routine. The tuck shop continued in business and although there was food rationing, there is little recollection of real hardship.

The regiments were anxious to recruit officers for the continuing war and would send representatives to the College – a Major Cave was especially active for the 60th Rifles, but a memorable visit was made by Major General Blakiston-Houston on behalf of the 27th Lancers. A selected band assembled in a small room. 'My name is Blakiston-Houston' began the General. 'The Commanding Officer is Horsbrough-Porter – right, bring your bums to rest.' After a time the head boy of Radley cautiously raised his hand. 'Please, sir, is it expensive to be an officer in the regiment?' Like a thunderclap came the answer – 'Depends what you spend on the women and the best will not cost you much anyway.'

The College buildings at Eastbourne were occupied by the Navy and in the latter stages of the war the College cricket team would return to play their hosts on the College ground. However the peaceful setting would be interrupted by a light AA gun mounted on the College tower, which periodically fired a few shots to make sure it was in working order. Petrol was rationed and in very short supply, so that most of the sports teams travelled by rail, the annual cricket match against Lancing taking place on Worcester county ground.

As the war went on into 1943 we began to hear of old boys who had recently been at the College but who had been killed. We also read letters from elder brothers at the front. The black-out continued but the bombing raids became less frequent as the Germans diverted their resources to the East.

Relations between the two schools remained surprisingly good and this was because we worked together and the headmaster, FJ Nugee, was an old Radleian. This good spirit is now commemorated by a plaque at Radley to recall the war years in which Eastbournians shared the same buildings as Radleians.

In 1945, by the time the College returned to Eastbourne, numbers were down to about 120. My brother never returned to Eastbourne but spent his five years in the College at Radley – one of the small band of Eastbournians to do so. I left in 1943 – to join the 27th Lancers.

David Sheldon (Crosby 1939)

After about fifty years, it is difficult to know how accurate one's recollections are! However I have a few, though I think they are rather trivial.

I entered the College (Crosby) in May 1939 and my only memory of our evacuation train to Radley was a venture into the unknown and that the train kept on stopping! Being a junior, we were sent to Nuneham Park and of that I remember even less.

I still have a letter written by my mother from Crowborough where we lived and dated June 20th 1940, the actual date of the evacuation. She writes:

> It is just five minutes to eleven and I am picturing you all in the train ready to leave Eastbourne, I expect with mixed feelings: but please God, I trust it will only be for a short time. You will be glad now the move is over as it must have been a strenuous move for everyone. I wonder if you had the Air Raid Warnings last night and the night before. It lasted here for four hours last night and three quarters of an hour the night before and how that beastly siren wailed and wailed. I thought of you and it made me all the more pleased to think you were going. I don't expect in any case you slept too well on the floor but must try and realise it

is all an experience. I hope you will soon settle down in your new abode. Now you will be in a mansion. Lord Harcourt is the name of the owner.

We got the HM's instructions and very good and sensible they were. I feel very sorry for him.

Now about your bike! We think it much better if you try and get on without it this term and you don't even know what you want it for yet. We think it would cost at least 10/- or 15/- to send it by passenger train and then it might quite easily get smashed. We really do think you might do without it this term unless you need it for school duties.

I really am glad to think you are going to Oxford and we know that part quite well though not actually Nuneham Park.

I can't remember if I managed to do without a bike for that first term, but I do remember, later on, using my bike to go to Oxford to the theatre and concerts, and it was during this time that I learnt to appreciate classical music.

Country runs were quite a feature, but on the whole I enjoyed them as I have always appreciated the countryside and it was beautiful round Radley.

Crosby House 1940

Back row: PA Houghton, JF Brooks, AR Davey, DL Sheldon, HM Spanton, CCG Tufton, MH Russell
Second row: MLJ Marshall, GE Michell, CD Gwyther, JF Dixon-Nuttall, PL Sibree, PKN Lister, ??, JTP Neild
Seated: Miss Young, RJG Weeks, Mrs Bagnall-Oakeley, Hugo Bagnall-Oakeley, Mr HK Bagnall-Oakeley, BC Stigant, AW Halfhide, Mr RRW Simpson
Seated on ground: CPA Walter, HM Benians, BOL Duke, J Thomas, PFV Stigant, GWD Chittenden
Inset: TRM Sewell, GAA Johanson

The Chapel Services stand out quite well in my mind and I had to read lessons in them during my last term (Lent 1943), as I was a school prefect. I remember that the Radleians always wore their gowns for chapel, but we didn't have them and wore jackets. One of our services was a BBC broadcast; I believe it was shortly after our evacuation.

Heading to the chapel was a long cloister and I still have a list of members who wished to attend a Natural History Society meeting. This must have been in the Lent term of 1943 when I was secretary.

A few other vague recollections are watching the Oxford v. Cambridge boat race which was rowed nearby and I passed what I think was called Certificate A while I was in the Corps. Little did I know then that this training was a preparation for my fighting in the Coldstream Guards from Nijemen to Cuxhaven towards the end of the war. Finally I used to listen to a little Bakelite wireless and hear on it interesting war news. Sometimes I used to wonder whether I would be called up.

Paul Walter (Crosby/Wargrave/Blackwater 1939)

In 1941, after the Phoney War I suppose, I decided to keep a diary and if I leaf through these diaries there must be masses of things which will spring to mind again. I of course took part in the evacuation and was on the special train, but being only in the Junior School went to Nuneham Park for the rest of the summer 1940. I have photographs of tennis being played there and of the house. You could still get film up to 1941. The following term we all went to Radley and the Crosby Prep Room was in the attic of the music school. They now have a splendid little concert hall built on to the old music school and the whole building has been modernised.

Crosby House 1941

Back row: BOL Duke, HM Benians, MH Vickery, J Thomas, CPA Walter
Second row: DL Sheldon, MH Russell, MLJ Marshall, AR Davey, CCG Tufton, HM Spanton
Seated: Miss Young, PL Sibree, HKN Lister, Mr HK Bagnall-Oakeley, JF Dixon-Nuttall, Mr RRW Simpson
Seated on ground: GWD Chittenden, JRB Clarke, MJC Haines, PFV Stigant

Things I remember – bicycles being allowed; marvellous! Blue paint on rear mudguards for Eastbourne and red for Radley.

Frequent trips with leave chits to Abingdon or Oxford.

Buying eggs at the farm on the Abingdon Road.

Learning to skate in the hard winter of 1942 on the gravel pits, also on the Warden's lake.

The BBC broadcast a service of ours from the chapel. Also Malcolm Sargent came to Radley in 1941, 23rd May – the day HMS *Hood* was sunk – conducted the London Philharmonic Orchestra, and made a speech telling us how lucky we were! We didn't think so at the time – or not many of us.

Then there were those whole holidays on Ascension Day and Lady Day which Radley always had had, so they were forced to give them to us too.

I seem to remember punting on the Cherwell.

Crosby House 1942

Back row: PFV Stigant, J Thomas, BOL Duke, HM Benians, MH Vickery, GWD Chittenden, DL Sheldon, MJC Haines, CPA Walter, JRB Clarke
Seated: Miss Young, MLJ Marshall, MH Russell, Mr HK Bagnall-Oakeley, CCG Tufton, HM Spanton, Mr TWM Halliday
Seated on ground: ??, ??, ??

The Chaplain was a chap called Gilfillan and we called him 'Sackcloth'. I learnt later that he was a New Zealander and Nugee said to me after I had left: 'I don't know what you boys did to him.' He was succeeded of course by Charles Neate – a very kind and sensitive man.

I remember the art master Paul Feiler. I believe he is still going strong down in the West Country somewhere. I once asked him how you became a Royal Academician – and of course he did become one. His reply to me was 'I shall be an R.A. one day.' I see from my diary of 1st May 1943 that he had had two pictures accepted for the summer exhibition that year.

The clubs and societies carried on – I became Hon. Sec. Web. Soc. before I left.

I don't remember very much of Wick Hall except a severe notice on the wall of the washroom: 'Please wash your hands on the soap, not on the towel!' Presumably put there by VMA's mother.

This had been only a brief sketch – a more detailed one from putting up the black-out in 1939 at Ascham to my returning to Eastbourne with the 1st XI (as scorer!) at the end of the summer of 1944, could be the work of weeks. We were the guests of the Navy (HMS *Marlborough*) and they gave us a right royal reception. We each had a programme typed out in naval language, 'muster at ... at ... hours' etc., etc. and ending with a visit at their expense to the Winter Gardens to see *The Merry Widow*.

VMA says in his book that no evacuated boy returned, but for years it was rumoured that one boy did, namely Stan Halstead (School House 1940). Only a look at the blue book for Michaelmas Term 1945 would prove this.

[He did not. Ed.].

Duncan Allan (Powell 1940)

We were lucky because Pennell and Powell houses were given a proper house [formerly 'H' Social] quite near the clock tower and tuck shop. Others were housed in the most peculiar places. One house was billeted above the music school and had to endure boys practising various musical instruments for hours on end and the bugle band marching up and down.

While our living quarters were excellent, it was always cold and everybody had chilblains. The food was appalling but nevertheless we ate absolutely everything that was put in front of us and there were no second helpings. There was a war on and everything was rationed or in short supply. Pocket money was spent almost exclusively on food. For some reason plum jam was not rationed and we bought it from the tuck shop and spread it on bread stolen from the dining room. Home cooking on the gas rings was a daily necessity, the ingredients being powdered egg, peanut butter, margarine, bread and plum jam.

Mr Storrs was our house master and willy nilly, like it or not, I was put in the science classes unwillingly learning physics and chemistry when my liking was for history and English literature. There was a war on and one had to learn something useful. I did flourish in the Corps, rising to sergeant. We wore First World War uniforms with puttees and peaked hats. As far as I can remember we never actually fired our rifles but I had the use of a 16 bore shot gun and a 22 rifle, lent to me by the local farmer's son at Chalk Farm, to shoot rabbits on my holidays – my main source of pocket money on holiday.

I had been taught to box at prep school in Eastbourne so that was a sport that I enjoyed. Being small and bossy, Mr Storrs took me from cricket, at which I was quite good, and made me a cox. I loved the Thames at Radley and fondly remember the balmy days of summer along the tow path. It was just like the *Wind in the Willows*.

I did not really know what to do with myself at the age of seventeen. I passed my School Certificate, only just, since I took subjects in which I had no real interest, until a retired General gave us a lecture on the Indian Army. I knew immediately what I wanted to do. Thus

I attended the Indian Military Academy, was commissioned with 1st Gurkha Rifles and, after partition, became a tea planter. I was well taught at Eastbourne, but all the wrong subjects!

Peter A Homburger (School House 1942)

I remember the old clock tower. Only school prefects could walk by it. Everyone else had to walk on the narrow side.

Being a school server and moving those heavy trollies with all the dishes etc. from the kitchen to the hall where Eastbourne College ate their meals.

In that same hall, using a knife to flick pats of margarine up to the ceiling and wondering during what auspicious occasion the drips would start to fall on unsuspecting people.

Going to the farm across from Gonville (the old vicarage) and being able to buy one egg a month.

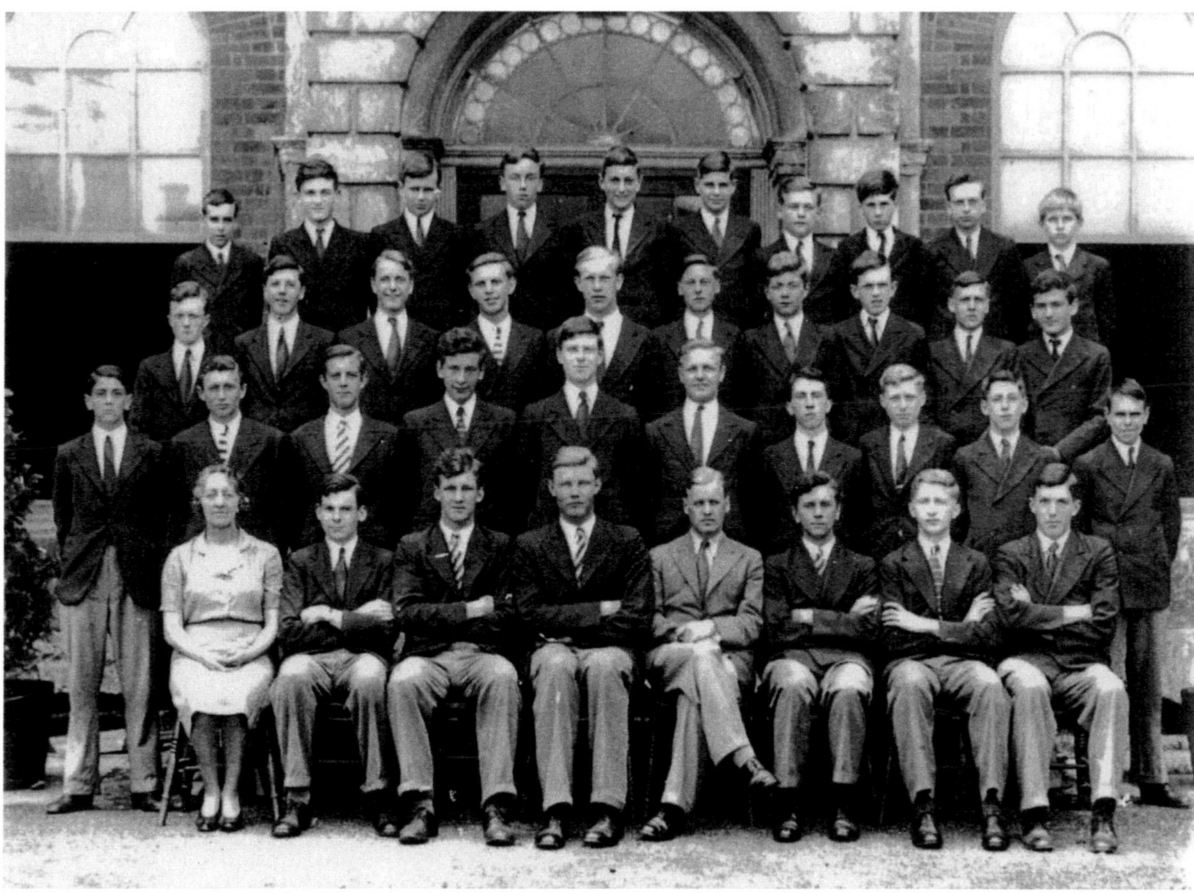

School House 1942

Back row: AL Hall, PA Homburger, PJ Halfhide, PJ Mathew, R Vaughan, DA Percival, MA Wadman, Dunn?, T Harington, GM Clayton
Second row: TFD Oram, J Oecken, DS Sams, P Spickernell, WH Eliot, DL Hudson, EG Learner, W Lloyd George, IB McDougall, WS Homburger
Third row: JAC Streeten, KH Watson?, NRF MacKinnon, J Pope, JG Essame, S Halstead, RF Macdonald, AC Foxley, JN Balmford, ??
Seated: Mrs Young, AR Bonner, AW Shaw, BTY Pegg, Mr HJ Belk, DA Tytler, RK Thompson, GDB Pearse

Using an old tin can, filling it with orange rind and saccharine and water and making marmalade over the fire in the prep room of School House (the entrance hall of the big mansion).

Having Revd Hope for maths and having to do mental arithmetic at the beginning of every class.

Having air raid drills where the 'injured' wore luggage tags to explain their injuries. We also wore gasmasks. In one exercise, lying in the coal cellar, the gasmask was yanked off then the tag was read – 'dislocated jaw'. (Donated by my brother Wolfgang.)

John L Johnstone (Gonville 1944)

I joined Gonville House September 1944. Two other late starters commenced with me – Eric Dynes (Gonville 1944) and James Watt (Gonville 1944). We had our study area over the entrance, where if we were careful we could use headsets connected to the radiators to hear the news. Some of the members of the house lived in the Rectory, down by the school gates.

About once a term a group of us would be off school work for a week whilst we helped in the kitchens washing up. The two schools had separate dining rooms. Games areas were separate.

Some of the older boys were involved with the home guard. All other boys were in the various cadet formations – Army, Navy or Air Force. The School had a Corps Band which practised on the games pitch.

I can remember being taught Chemistry by a Miss Jordan (a teacher from Radley) – I think we were a group from both schools. Most of us had bicycles, so we were able to go into Abingdon and the surrounding area.

At half term quite a number of boys were taken to Oxford by their parents. Our main rivals at games were Radley, St Edwards (Oxford), Lancing and Tonbridge. We were 'encouraged' to take part in the yearly cross country which was set around the Radley area. Invariably it seemed to rain before, during or after or all three. We weren't disturbed by bombs or air raids while at Radley.

Gonville House 1944

Back row: PD Edwards?, CM Harvey-Cook, AM Lermit?, AR Wilson, RM Barwell, AM Fife-Miller, G Hornby, IR McNaught, VPC Whitamore
Second row: AE Broad?, ??, TR Colgate, GEH Wilson, RN Horne, ??, JA Hebditch, JN Horne, ??, ES Overy
Seated: Matron, ??, BEN Lyte, Mr RG Howell, AC Morrison, ??, ??, RFB Speed, ??
Seated on ground: BE Cole, TN Smallman, C Leyland-Naylor, MD Read, JA Shepherd, JM Atkins

Wargrave House 1942
Back row: DED Foster, SE Sylvester, JR Turner-Ettlinger, RJM Roberts, ES Overy, AJS Watson, MF Tollitt, RH Walker, DG Hall
Seated: JWPB McIntosh, JP Davis, Mr VM Allom, WA Lawson, PD Burdett
Seated on ground: GF Alexander, AM Lermit

Blackwater House 1943
Back row: DC Scott?, MF Hudson, FR Hall, BDO Smith, MJC Haines, JRB Clarke, AV Dunlop, DJ Halfhide, DB Holtom, GG Sadler
Second row: AHM Shaw, KD Sandberg, CPA Walter, RH Newman, GWD Chittenden, J Thomas, P Milton Thompson, PFV Stigant
Seated: MJM Lea, JC Lindsay, BOL Duke, FJ Venn, Mr RC Burton, MH Vickery, ??, Miss Hayhoe
Seated on ground: JJ Raper, A Carter, GH Bilton, KLT Tugwell

School House 1945
Back row: J Lock, M Vaughan, JM Curtis, BH Whitmore, WJ Millns, HCB Overbury, A de C True, P Hall, I Dawson, AR Gleed
Second row: AL Hall, CAM Walkeley, JC Bevan, GM Clayton, KB Barton, CFK Dunn, DA Lethem, GIH Traill, JD Johnston
Third row: JPE Parry Okeden, MA Wadman, PA Homburger, PJ Halfhide, PJ Mathew, R Vaughan, JW Wills, PAM Allan, JH Vinnicombe, GS Goodsir
Seated: DS Sams, Mrs Young, EG Learner, S Halstead, Mr HJ Belk, TFD Oram, W Lloyd George, AC Foxley, J Oecken

Blackwater House 1945
Back row: D Matson, KG Sainsbury, CJ Pickford, RB Haythornthwaite, KB Stone, DO'S Hoare, PM Clarke, PB Sandford-Johnson, CR Raper, JC Robbins, AG New
Second row: PD Brauen, VD Brice, A (Carter) Graham, GH Bilton, BDO Smith, P Allen, G Milton Thompson, KL Tugwell, CR Sacré
Seated: Miss Hayhoe, JJ Raper, P Milton Thomson, Mr RC Burton, FR Hall, AV Dunlop
Seated on ground: AG Fisher, AFS Lester, AI Gosnell, N Auton

The Great Game
College v. Radley
Played on Radley 'Big Side' on 11 November 1944
Won 4–3

Beefy Howell's Match Report

Though our side was considerably depleted, the absence of Spickernell being particularly grievous, we started briskly and it was soon obvious that our team meant to put up a great fight. The weather made the ball difficult to handle and Wilson wisely changed the tactics and ordered Bell to kick.

By shrewd kicking Bell was able to regain all the ground Radley won by their handling and dribbling. Horne and Wilson both made promising runs, but half-time came without any score.

We started the second half with only seven forwards as Sadler had most unfortunately dislocated his arm just before half-time. A number of dangerous runs were launched by the Radley three-quarters, but fortunately our tackling, falling and covering was grand. Every man was brought down and Watson cleared splendidly every time, until in trying to stop a forward rush, the ball slipped away at the last moment and Radley dribbled over for a try (0–3). Fortunately our team refused to be disheartened, and the forwards grandly let by Williamson and Halstead proceeded to heel the ball as well as doing some fine rushes, while

The Great Game 1944

Touch Judge, DS Sams, RN Horne, MJC Haines, GEH Wilson, KH Watson, P Spickernell (non-playing captain), GG Sadler, AS Hunt, S Halstead, RB Harrison, JG Essame, AD Mitchell, CC Brown, DA Bell (AV Dunlop absent)

Bell's touch kicking always made useful ground. Wilson and his outsides, ably assisted by some very fine tackles by Haines, nipped every Radley counter-move in the bud. Bell's kicking and a dribble by Brown took us to the Radley '25', where Wilson made a strong burst, but was overwhelmed by numbers. A scrum was formed under the Radley posts, the forwards heeled beautifully and Harrison passed straight back to Bell for the latter to drop a magnificent goal (4–3). Another 15 minutes now remained for play, and both sides went all out. Frantic efforts were made, efforts which aroused the enthusiasm of all the spectators, but we hung grimly on to our slender lead and won a most memorable victory.

It was a grand effort by the whole team, everyone doing his utmost. The weather was undoubtedly in our favour, but our team deserves every credit for the way they overcame their misfortunes and refused to admit defeat. It was a great game to watch, played throughout with great determination, but in an excellent spirit.

And Robin Harrison's memory of the game:

As a young Colt recently promoted to the 1st XV I still remember well a dank, mid-November day in 1944 on Radley Big Side, with the rain sweeping down the ground driven by a strong wind. It was towards the end of the war and our period of evacuation to Radley, and our numbers had shrunk to just 162. Yet, under the inspired coaching of Beefy Howell we were still unbeaten that year as we faced a superb Radley side who had been sweeping all before them. In an earlier match we had lost one of our best forwards with a dislocated knee, a centre with a broken finger, and worst of all we were without our captain and fly half, Peter Spickernell, who was injured just a few days before the match. 'Buster' Bell, a temperamental wing three-quarter but a fine kicker, was brought in to play fly half.

I well remember the massed ranks of the Radley supporters on one side of the pitch and their rather feeble bleat of 'Radley, Radley, Radley' completely drowned by the full-throated roar of 'College' coming from our depleted ranks on the other side, though outnumbered three or four to one. Just before half time our wing forward GG Sadler broke his arm and, as there were no substitutes in those days, we had to face the wind and the rain in the second half with only 14 men. I remember little of the game itself except slithering around in the mud, tackling and falling, falling and tackling, and Bell's superb touchline kicking which kept waves of cerise and white jerseys at bay as they swept down to our line again and again. Eventually they scored a try, but soon after, on just about our only visit to their '25' in the entire game, we won a scrum under the Radley posts and Bell dropped a fine goal into the teeth of the wind. In those days a try was worth three points and a drop-goal four, so we won a titanic struggle 4–3 and I am told that tears were streaming down Beefy's face at the end. A most unworthy victory, you may say, by today's scoring. But all who saw that epic game, both Radley and Eastbourne alike, recognize it as symbolic of the spirit of Eastbourne which kept the College going as our numbers shrank and shrank through those grim wartime years of evacuation. Whenever I meet Radley masters or Old Boys who saw the match, they mention it still.

The 1944 Stags

Standing: Mr RG Howell, DM Scrimgeour, RN Horne, GA Irwin, JG Essame, AS Hunt, KH Watson, AD Mitchell

Seated: MJC Haines, DB Tanqueray, GEH Wilson, P Spickernell, S Halstead, CC Brown, GG Sadler

Seated on ground: DA Bell, RB Harrison

Cricket and Rugby at Radley

Eastbourne and Radley 1st XIs 1942
Back row: RL Anstruther (E), DE Mathews (R), ?? (E), IDW Sawtell (R), MH Russell (E), RC Lucas (R)
Second row: PH McCalman (E), NC Laing (R), NRM Philcox (E), JFS Agar (R), BLG Beeson (E), JV Edwards (R), BEN Lyte (E), MJD Syson (R)
Seated: PA Chard (E), LM Barker (R), Mr RC Burton (E), Mr Borgris (R), AB Curtis (E), AG Gardner (R)
Seated on ground: RAE Wilson (E), MB Parry-Crooke (R), JMA Gunn (R), BG Luard (E)

2nd XI 1944

Rugby 1st XV 1940–1
Back row: Mr RG Howell, RS Marshall, HC Parsons, WIH Gwynne-Jones, AI Keith-Fraser, GP Syme-Thomson
Seated: RL Anstruther, AB Curtis, DG Dickson, KB Mackenzie (Capt), PA Chard, AG Bryan-Brown, HMR Newton
Seated on ground: P Donaldson, BLG Beeson, ND Paine

Rugby 2nd XV 1941–2
Back row: HM Spanton, DJ Griffin, MS Scrimgeour, CWH Williams, AD McNaught, PL Sibree, JP Davis, AEV Wadman, PFL Mills
Seated: TWA Glenister, PJ Elton, SR Duncan (Capt), JF Dixon-Nuttall, N Lea-Cox
Seated on ground: DM Hancock, AW Goodinge, DA Tytler

Rugby 1st XV 1942–3
Back row: Mr RG Howell, JD Simson?, BA Beaumand?, BT Pegg, RS Marshall, Hon KHL Lamb, PA de Havilland, Inset: AB Curtis
Seated: ??, RL Anstruther, PA Chard, BLG Beeson,??
Seated on ground: MH Russell, JS Fry, IDM Mackenzie?
Unidentified: P Donaldson, MLJ Marshall, JBW Goodwin

Rugby 2nd XV 1944–5

Eastbourne College – Eastbourne Branch
A Memoir by the Acting Headmaster, HK Bagnall-Oakeley
Gonville 1942–45

During the summer term of 1942 we heard that Eastbourne College was to reopen one house back at Eastbourne. The school governors were worried that if they waited until the end of the war it might be impossible to restart the College after an absence of so many years and they were being urged by the town council to reopen as a day school since a number of school age boys had no school to go to. The Ministry of Defence, who had taken over all the College buildings in 1940, agreed to release one house – Gonville – and the headmaster asked me to take a small team back to Eastbourne and reopen the school in September 1942. My colleagues were Vin Allom and David Craig. Vin was a bachelor who lived with his elderly mother and possessed independent means derived from a family business. He was a fine schoolmaster who could teach almost any subject; he was also a tall, striking looking man who resembled a classical actor and had a booming voice. Vin had one or two mild eccentricities – for instance he wore a monocle and was an habitual snuff taker. He was an exceptionally kind and understanding person with a deep understanding of the psyche of schoolboys and he was a devout Christian. David Craig was another outstanding schoolmaster who became a very successful housemaster after the war. After his tragically early death from cancer one of the new houses was named Craig House in his memory. David was married to Joyce, the sister of Robert Storrs, and they had seven children, two of whom died in infancy. David was principally a maths teacher but he could turn his hand to most subjects when required. On our return to Eastbourne Evelyn and I moved into Gonville with Nanny and the children. Vin Allom and his mother took a house [Clovelly Cottage in Blackwater Road] near the College buildings and the Craigs lived further up Carlisle Road. Most of the large Edwardian houses in this part of the town were unoccupied, their owners having moved away from the south coast for the duration of the war. Chelmsford Hall, a prep school on the other side of Carlisle Road, was occupied by the Royal Navy and we were able to use its playing field which was diagonally opposite Gonville.

During the summer holidays we advertised in the local papers that the College was reopening and invited prospective parents to come and see us. By the beginning of the Michaelmas term of 1942 we had a total of 16 pupils but numbers steadily increased and the Governors then asked me if we could start taking prep school age boys. I replied that neither I nor my colleagues had any experience of teaching boys in the 8 to 13 age group but we would do our best if I could be allowed to recruit an additional member of staff who could concentrate on the younger boys. We were fortunate in being able to secure the services of Miss Howlett who took charge of our juniors. The Governors had decided to establish a junior school after the war and this moved into the former Ascham building where I had been housemaster for less than a year in 1938/9. Later the Governors asked us to take boarders.

Evelyn was fully committed organising the catering – as well as bringing up our children – so I was allowed to recruit a matron, Mrs Rose, whose late husband had been a colonel in the Gurkhas and whose son Hugh was later to come to the College. Somehow Vin, David and I managed between us to teach all the usual subjects except Greek and in 1945, the last year of the war, every boy passed every subject he took in the School Certificate! One boy had actually failed all seven subjects he had entered while at the Grammar School and then passed them all as soon as he came to us. I suspect that the examiners were less demanding during the war because of the difficult conditions and frequent disruptions in schools: certainly we were asked to record and report to the authorities every interruption to lessons – or the boarders' sleep – caused by air raids and so on. In fact the town of Eastbourne had no

Eastbourne College, Eastbourne Branch 1945

Standing: GP Meanley, SD Morris, DJM Caffyn, J Sogno, TW Patton, S Stock, MT Langdon, ??, RA Moss, RN Bones, S Hubbard-Ford, CM Turner, J Penn, ??, RJM Caffyn, ADH Higman, PB Hetherington, H Rose, AA Mackintosh, PJ Beckett, IMD McAuley, TJB Bawden, JJD Price, AG Robbins, LLI Botcherby, CMK Taylor

Second row: DH Botcherby, C Kerridge, A James, JL Wheeler, GA Hetherington, ??, ID Sykes, PJ Grant, PD Attenborough, CK Humphryes, RG Holloway, RA Bell, JL Arnold, Wymark?, CH Hamilton, T Pescud, AM Caffyn, J Perrin, LT Turle, GR Thornton, ??, ??, JG Binns, GJD Price, BT Pearson, RL Mitchell, MF A'Brook, ??

Seated: A Strong, BC Douglas-Hamilton, MTH Clark, JH Brissenden, PA Seager, WH Ward, J Pumphrey, JPT Holloway, AW Levett, Mrs Rose, EH Toovey, ??, Mr TD Craig, Mrs Bagnall-Oakeley, Charmian, MrHK Bagnall-Oakeley, Hugo, Mr VM Allom, Miss Howlett, Mr EH McCormick, Mrs McCormick, DL Stevens, Mrs Housden, MH Collings, GA Adamson, DJ Turle, SH Boniface, RJ Beckett, BD Graham, DA Urch, JH Vincent

strategic importance to the enemy as it was a largely depopulated residential area. There were no port facilities, airfields or large factories and most of the bombs were dropped by enemy aircraft retreating from targets further inland and small groups of raiders who crossed the Channel – often at low level – then did a quick straffing run and fled back out to sea. Altogether the town suffered about 30 raids after our return – this excludes attacks by 'doodlebugs' or flying bombs and the V2 rockets which were aimed at London but sometimes went off course – and the worst individual incident was when the public library was destroyed by a large bomb or landmine causing a number of casualties. On one occasion Nanny was walking down Carlisle Road with Hugo when a Messerschmit 110 came over the Downs just north of Beachy Head and flew down the road at rooftop height with guns blazing. Nanny put Hugo over the wall of a front garden and stood in the road shaking her fist and giving the pilot a piece of her mind. Hugo was most indignant as he particularly wanted to get a close view of a ME110: he also liked to rush out into the streets after a raid and collect pieces of shrapnel, preferably still hot. We wouldn't allow him to go out until the all clear had sounded and this irked him because his friend Stephen Stock, who lived opposite, was allowed out earlier. I once found Nanny heating some shrapnel and spent cannon shells under the grill before emptying them in the road just outside our front door for Hugo to find!

I was an air-raid warden for the immediate area – I think that my 'beat' covered about 40 houses, most of which were unoccupied. By 1942 everyone's blackout was in place and the wardens no longer needed to go round shouting 'put that light out!'; the main job was to go round after a raid to extinguish any incendiaries. In the summer we sometimes picnicked in the garden of an empty house for which I was responsible. Food – or rather the lack of it – was a constant preoccupation as the war went on. I kept hens in an enclosure at the end of what had been Gonville's back garden (it was now a tarmac playground) and often shot pigeons as they came over. There were comparatively few immediate neighbours and most of

them were service personnel; besides, in 1942–5 people were fairly used to hearing bangs. I once shot a pigeon which fell in the road just as a naval detachment was parading in front of Chelmsford Hall. I didn't want to lose it so I dropped the gun and sauntered out with a trug basket, pretended to notice it for the first time and rushed over to clear it away from in front of the parade! Another pigeon that I shot while it was perched on the chimney pot of a nearby house fell down the chimney but fortunately the house was unoccupied and I found the rather sooty bird in the fireplace. I also rented an allotment on the edge of the Downs above St Andrew's prep school (this area is now a housing estate) and grew a variety of vegetables. One summer's day I was up there with Hugo when some enemy aircraft crossed the coast and headed inland. They did not attack Eastbourne but they did attract an intense barrage of AA and shell fragments started falling around us like hail. There was no shelter for some distance so I turned a small metal water tank on its side and put Hugo inside it: he was then a small, skinny five year old. The tank was too small for me and Hugo was anxious that I should also take shelter: he was not convinced when I proposed covering my head with a cabbage leaf so I eventually compromised by sticking my head in the tank. In the summer of 1944 we had a grandstand view from the allotment as swarms of V1s flew across the coast and our AA and fighters tried to shoot them down. We could see the puffs of smoke from shell bursts surround a doodlebug, followed by a brilliant flash as one was hit: then, a few seconds later, a big thud as the noise of the explosion reached us. Hugo has since told me that this was when he first realised that sound travelled far slower than light. Perhaps an even better sight was when we saw a Typhoon fly right up to a V1, turn it round with its wingtip and send it back out to sea. Eastbourne was packed with troops in the weeks before D Day and although security was absolute it was obvious that the invasion was imminent. All the long straight streets were lined with tanks, guns and vehicles of every kind. A good proportion of these troops were Canadians and during the days of waiting they often practised lacrosse. I had only seen lacrosse played by schoolgirls and I was amazed at the distance these Canadians could pass the ball to one another. Unfortunately some of the Canadians were pretty wild and there was considerable drunkenness, looting and violence before they left for Normandy, but the Naval sentries at Chelmsford Hall always looked after us and removed drunk Canadians from our premises before they could do any harm. All the troops were very kind to the children and often gave them sweets. Just before D Day our troops were ordered to take all their sports equipment to be burned in the Council's refuse destructor. Many of the footballs, cricket bats etc were brand new and I don't know which genius at the MOD issued the order but one unit who we had got to know disobeyed; they had been digging slit trenches in one of the gardens where I had my bee hives and after they left I noticed that one of these trenches had been filled in. Just below the surface I found a pile of new sports equipment and tins of spare food which they had left for us.

During the last few months of the war we had few air raids but the V1s came over from June 1944 until the Allies overran their launch sites during September. The V2 rockets continued to be launched from Holland until about March 1945 but they were aimed at London and only one landed in Eastbourne as far as I am aware.

Eastbourne Branch boarders 1945

Back row: IMD McAuley, JJD Price, DJ Humphryes, KT Roberts, RL Mitchell, PCH Farmer, JA Penn, PF Wright

Second row: H Rose, GR Thornton, GJD Price, BT Pearson, JG Binns, RG Holloway, AM James, AG Robbins

Seated: Mrs C Rose, Mrs Bagnall-Oakeley, Mr HK Bagnall-Oakeley, Miss AR Howlett, Mrs Housden

Seated on ground: Charmian, Hugo

VE day in May 1945 was a public holiday and our day boys stayed at home. We decided to take the boarders for a picnic on the beach below Beachy Head. We walked up to St Bede's school and then along the cliffs to Cow Gap where we got down on to the beach and walked along it towards the lighthouse. This was quite safe because a friend of mine who repaired the telephone line to the lighthouse whenever it was severed by low flying aircraft (trying to get below our radar) had told me where the minefields were. The beach had hardly been visited for six years and we found huge cockles, whelks, shrimps and a plentiful supply of driftwood with which to make a fire. Meanwhile Evelyn and Mrs Rose had carried food on their bikes as far as Cow Gap and we had a splendid picnic. The highlight was the sudden appearance of a German submarine; it transpired that all enemy submarines had been ordered to surface near an Allied vessel, make black smoke and wait to be boarded. This particular sub evidently couldn't find a ship to which it could surrender so the captain decided to surrender to the lighthouse but the local paper, the *Eastbourne Gazette*, reported that it had surrendered to a schoolmaster and a party of boys! We carried on as normal for the rest of the summer term 1945 and during the holidays the rest of the College returned from Radley. Gonville was taken over by Ronald Howell, and I was to re-start Crosby, together with the adjoining Wargrave, as soon as the buildings were released by the services and re-equipped as boarding houses. Meanwhile we moved into a flat in Silverdale Road which had been occupied by Evelyn's mother during the last part of the war.

Eastbourne College, Eastbourne Branch, 1940–45

First published in the *Old Eastbournian* in 2005

by Michael Clark, Eastbourne Branch and Powell House 1942–48

Michael Clark

For many OEs the above title may appear something of an enigma. To enlighten the puzzled, one must consider the situation in Eastbourne in June 1940. The British Expeditionary Force had been driven from France; German forces were massed across the channel; invasion seemed imminent. John Nugee, the Headmaster, and the Governors decided that it was imperative that the College should evacuate. The urgent need to find a suitable location for the College's wartime sojourn could have caused problems.

Fortunately a swift solution came to hand. Radley College in Oxfordshire made arrangements for the College to move there to share their facilities. This generous and unselfish offer by the Warden (headmaster) of Radley College was facilitated by the fact that John Nugee had had a long and distinguished career there, being Sub-Warden prior to his appointment as Headmaster of Eastbourne. In spite of difficulties, e.g. cramming a quart of students into a pint pot, the boys settled down well together. In the Spring term of 1942 worrying rumours were circulating in Eastbourne; would the College survive the war to return to Eastbourne? There was another factor to be considered: requests were being received for quality education in Eastbourne. Roborough, the last of the independent schools to survive, was about to close down. The Headmaster and Council had to consider the viability of opening a day boy house in Eastbourne. Ultimately the decision was made to proceed. At the time, the College premises were occupied by HMS *Marlborough*, a Royal Naval shore establishment (torpedo training). The Admiralty granted the College the right to take over one of the houses. It was initially envisaged that, being a day boy house, it would be Powell. However, the CO of HMS *Marlborough*, Capt TG Jackson RN, turned this down on security grounds. He wished that the College central campus be enclosed as an entity by Navy-occupied buildings. After further negotiations, the College was allocated the Gonville House building. The official title was to be Eastbourne College, Eastbourne Branch. Three masters were sent down from Radley to run the Branch. HK Bagnall-Oakeley was in charge, ably assisted by VM Allom and TD Craig. After a while it became evident that many of the boys seeking admission were of prep school, rather than public school, age. To deal with this unexpected situation Miss AR Howlett and a part-time master were recruited to join the teaching staff.

Kemeys Bagnall-Oakeley was nicknamed 'Bags'. He taught geography and science, exuded fitness and was the epitome of good health. He had a cheerful countenance coupled with good nature. As 'Headmaster' he was scrupulously fair and held in great respect. At Cambridge he had won a full Blue for athletics, he was an expert shot, an accomplished hockey player and a knowledgeable ornithologist. He ran the Eastbourne and District Spotters Club which trained members in aircraft recognition. In a darkened room, silhouettes of British, American and German aircraft were shone on a screen by means of an epidiascope. John Holloway and I were awarded certificates for proficiency in aircraft recognition. Bags was a great believer in physical fitness; in the morning break we were put through a vigorous regime of PT (PE). He arranged a hockey match against a team of WRNS from HMS *Marlborough*, played on the Chelmsford Hall prep school field opposite Gonville which was also leased to the Navy. This was a painful experience with balls flying high and low, hitting some of us in vulnerable parts of the anatomy. We drew one-all. He took older boys for 22 shooting. The rifles were 303

Lee-Enfields fitted with tubes to reduce them to 22 calibre, the object being to minimise the kick, but still to give the experience of handling a heavier firearm. He introduced some of us to carpentry, which stood us in good stead in the coming age of DIY. He sowed the seeds of participation in voluntary work. An example of this was moving furniture from bomb-damaged houses to places of safe storage. On one occasion John Brisenden and I were sent to retrieve a valuable collection of mounted butterflies from a house in St John's Road for safe-keeping by Bags. The direct route to Gonville was via the precipitously steep Granville Hill. We had descended half-way down the hill when the costermonger's barrow loaded with the display cabinets of butterflies went out of control. It crashed into the pillar box on the corner of Silverdale Road. By a miracle no damage was done. At weekends he took the younger boarders on nature rambles, stimulating a keen interest in the local flora and fauna. The Bagnall-Oakeleys' prankster son, Hugo, was once seen to creep into the Gonville yard skirting Granville Road, holding a portable gramophone in one hand and clutching a record in the other. Outside on the road a sergeant-major was drilling soldiers. Then Hugo proceeded to play the highly amusing recording of *The Laughing Policeman*, much to the fury of the sergeant-major and the troops' vain efforts to suppress their sniggering.

Eastbourne College, Eastbourne Branch Scout Group

Back row: AW Levett, PA Seager, MTH Clark, MH Collings, DL Stephens, ??, ??
Second row: P Hetherington, S Hubbard-Ford, JH Vincent, WH Ward, Wymark?, ??, JH Perrin?, CMK Taylor
Third row: JJD Price, IAG Snowball, CM Turner, JC Humphries, CH Hamilton, TJB Bawden, GA Hetherington, DA Urch, ??, MF A'Brook, RA Bell, ID Sykes, AM Caffyn, J Wheeler, IMD McAuley, BA Coulcher, TW Patton, GP Meanley
Fourth row: AA Mackintosh, DJM Caffyn, Mr McCullough, RN Bones, Mr VM Allom, RJM Caffyn, EH Toovey, SD Morris, S Stock

VM (Vincent Mulcaster) Allom was a tall distinguished-looking man, of upright stance, head held back. He displayed a hint of vanity, taking furtive glances at his reflection in mirrors or window panes. If he was particularly vexed he was given to an outburst of anger. This however soon melted away. He was a great sniffer of snuff, having unique brown handkerchiefs to camouflage the stains that would discolour white handkerchiefs. Vin taught English and French. However, his breadth and depth of knowledge, academic and general, was such that he had the capability of teaching any subject. He was also a gifted raconteur of stories of interest and amusement, a guarantee that the drowsiest individual would remain awake. He was proud of his ploy to safeguard the possible loss of his cheque book, as his cheques were printed 'VM Allom' above the section for his signature. However, his actual signature was V Mulcaster Allom. I don't think that this would offer much protection these days. Allom ran the Eastbourne College Scout Troop, leaders of which were David (Davo) Stevens and Michael Collings, the latter becoming a King's Scout. I have vivid memories of taking the Tenderfoot fire-lighting test on the scrub-like valley by Beachy Head Road overlooking Moira House School, now densely populated with a number of housing estates. He organised various wide games, for example the capture of a general behind enemy lines. Like Hitchcock, he would contrive to play a cameo role in the proceedings. In the summer holidays of 1945 a camp took place in the grounds of Wellington College in Berkshire, Vin being an old boy. On one morning, as was his wont, he went to the local newsagent to get the *Daily Telegraph* (the main crossword was completed in 15 minutes or less). On his return he was flushed and excited. 'The Americans have dropped an atomic bomb on Hiroshima.' We were mystified at the significance of it. 'Atomic bomb, what the heck is that?' Naïve and innocent youth, aware of some things but ignorant of others. The Eastbourne College Troop took part in the annual steeplechase across multi-ditched marshland stretching from the Neville House school cricket ground at the foot of King's Avenue, to almost as far as the present day District General Hospital. The course completed, participants emerged wet-through and besmirched with mud. Our team was victorious. We also took part in the scouts' swimming gala at Devonshire Baths, where we won the Eastbourne Shield. A group of boys from another troop caused a rumpus as the District Commissioner, Colonel Keen, was making an announcement. He was standing on a balcony, red in the face, his eyes bolting out of his head, apart from which he was a Baden-Powell look-alike. 'If you lads can't behave, I will clear the baths.' 'Absolutely no discipline!' he exclaimed, addressing a group of scoutmasters.

Allom was an air raid warden and was closely involved when an unexploded bomb came to rest in St Saviour's Church. He was a devotee of classical music, played the clarinet and sang alto. He had an antique wind-up gramophone which had an enormous papier-mâché horn. He always used fibre needles 'to produce the optimum quality of sound'. Besides, the metal needles damaged the records. He took us for musical appreciation. He taught us about the meanings of musical terminology, such as adagio, molto allegro, largo, scherzo, molto vivace, etc. He chose one of his favourite works, Dvorak's *Symphony No 9, From the New World*, to help illustrate theory. Listening to the recording of the symphony, we were expected to recognise the sound of musical instruments. Vin's trusty old gramophone was used to play the music. The sessions helped broaden the spectrum of musical taste which had been restricted to Tin Pan Alley (equivalent to *Top of the Pops*), Artie Shaw, Louis Armstrong, Glenn Miller, Harry Parry and other jazz and swing ensembles.

Vin's mother was a kind-hearted elderly lady of a motherly disposition. On a spring morning in 1945 she invited a number of us for a stroll along Grange Road. She cautioned us that on no account should we talk about it and that we should keep this a strict secret. Our curiosity was aroused; there was a distinct feeling that, in keeping with the wartime slogan 'careless talk costs lives', our meeting would be of a clandestine nature. At the appointed hour of 3pm, we kept our rendezvous with her with beating hearts and a keen anticipation as we gazed across College Field. After about ten minutes with no sign of anything happening, there were signs of impatience in our party. Mrs Allom, sensing the unrest, remarked tersely: 'You will not have much longer to wait.' All at once a low buzzing sound, punctuated by a persistent clatter, could be heard approaching through the air from the direction of the Town Hall.

A strange flying machine came into view. It had no wings, and appeared to have a large propeller-like blade rotating above its fuselage. It progressed to the centre of College field, where it hovered, slowly made a gentle vertical descent and a graceful landing. After a brief pause, two high-ranking naval officers clambered out. Of course, to the present generation it would be obvious that the aircraft was a helicopter. To us, it was a complete novelty of which we had never heard. It was one of the first to be operational in this country. The forerunner was the pre-war Autogiro, which had a comparatively poor performance.

Thomas David Craig, known to his colleagues as David, was affectionately referred to as 'Teddy' (when out of earshot). He had a ruddy complexion, his sleek black hair brushed straight back, and on his nose was perched a pair of gold-rimmed spectacles. In his pedestrian mode he had a rolling seafarer's gait; in his 'equestrian' mode he rode an ancient bicycle with a swaying motion to match his walk. He taught history and Latin. I detested Latin. However, it was deemed to be essential as I was destined to become a pharmacist (which involved dog-Latin). His history lessons were most absorbing and interjected with droll quips, mostly of a cynical nature. This tended to keep one awake, lest one missed his next amusing comment. He was given to sudden resounding outbursts in class, when a boy made a stupid mistake: 'You miserable creature', or what is now a politically unacceptable utterance, 'Cretin!'

Lt TD Craig, later promoted to Captain, could in some ways be compared to *Dad's Army*'s Captain Mainwaring. In September 1942, when the first corps parade took place, Teddy was the only one to have a uniform. It seemed that there was very little likelihood of them becoming available. The cadets, meanwhile, paraded in the scruffy utility clothing of the day. Craig had the idea of ringing up the bursar at Radley College to find out if there might be some uniforms left behind at Eastbourne. 'Yes, there could be some at Stanhope Court.' There were, indeed, some which turned out to be of First World War vintage, tunics with brass buttons, very wide webbing belts, caps and forage caps and puttees which could be likened to wide khaki bandages. These were in place of gaiters. They restricted the circulation to the lower legs and ankles, proved to be painful and could cause cramp. That left us without army boots, and so parents were prevailed upon to buy them. This request proved to be an unpopular one, as it was considered to be an unnecessary waste of precious clothing coupons. In due course we were issued with battledress, anklets, standard belts and berets.

Firstly, we drilled endlessly. We were told that this would enable us to respond instantly to words of command, this being essential when in combat. Then followed weapons training. The rifle was dealt with in-house. We were sent to the Court House, situated in a cul-de-sac off Moatcroft Road, just below the present day Safeway [now Waitrose] supermarket. This was a Home Guard headquarters where Colonel Tommy Sutton had his office and Company Sergeant-Major Jelley later taught us to strip and reassemble the Browning automatic rifle, the precursor of the Second World War Bren gun. Later, we were put through the same procedure for the mass-produced Sten gun, which was looked upon as the poor man's Tommy gun. Shortly after this we went to an improvised range just off Paradise Drive, near the Royal Eastbourne Golf Club, to practise shooting with the Sten gun. Each cadet was to shoot off a magazine of 9 mm bullets. An individual, who will remain anonymous, prepared to take his turn with the weapon, which was known to be unreliable. We stood well back behind the firing position. The cadet squeezed the trigger, nothing happened, so he turned round facing us, finger still on the trigger, making semi-circular movements in our direction. Instantly, we all threw ourselves flat on the ground, so illustrating the importance of the lessons learnt from the drilling.

Eastbourne College JTC, Eastbourne Platoon 1945

Back row: M Hickey, DA Urch, MF Boniface, BT Pearson, RJ Beckett, BC Douglas-Hamilton, JL Arnold, JH Perrin, BD Graham

Middle row: SH Boniface, JH Vincent, PA Seager, JH Brissenden, MTH Clark, AM Strong, JS Pumphrey, WH Ward, MC Whymark

Seated: GAH Samson, AW Levett, EH Toovey, Lt TD Craig, DL Stevens, MH Collings, JPT Holloway

Field days were very popular and were intended to put theory into practice. One field day involved the use of bicycles, a hare-brained idea to simulate Blitzkreig warfare. This ended in total chaos, with a broken bicycle frame, numerous broken spokes and greasy hands from chains that came adrift. We also had night operations. A mock skirmish was organised to take place around the remnants of a ruined mill above Paradise Plantation. The peaceful evening was shattered by the explosion of thunder flashes and the crackle of blanks. All of a sudden a policeman and an army officer appeared. 'Why hadn't the relevant authorities been informed of these exercises? It could have resulted in a serious incident.' The authorities had been notified of the night operations, but there had been a break-down in communications. In the holidays some cadets donned their uniforms and tried their luck to get into the Garrison Theatre, the peacetime Devonshire Park Theatre, where ENSA (Entertainments National Service Association) shows were put on for the Services. The ticket office girls must have realised we were rather young servicemen, but kindly turned a blind eye. The ultimate aim of the cadet training was to obtain Certificate A which was in two parts. It tested cadets in drill, field craft, map reading, weapons training, etc. It also called for a high standard of physical fitness. Those who obtained the full certificate were entitled to wear a red star-shaped insignia on the sleeve of their tunic.

Mrs Cecily Rose was the matron for the younger boys. She was a constantly cheerful young widow, who had a friendly but firm rapport with her charges, who were genuinely fond of her. Her son, Hugh, was at school in Gonville. Charles Wellbourne (Charlie Warlie), a smallish man with a slight stoop and white hair, had previously been head butler on the royal yacht. He seemed to be chiefly employed as a general factotum. He was principally seen at the time of the morning break when he served the staff coffee in the small common room on the back stairs. Vin Allom always seemed to be late for his refreshments, being earnestly in conversation with one boy or another. Wellbourne would be heard pleading with Vin, 'Mister Allum, yer koffee's gittin' kalud.' This seemed to be a source of irritation to him and he snapped back: 'Can't you see that I am busy, Charles?' There was a very large cook with enormous arms. She was of a jovial appearance, with a constant smile on her face.

The wartime years between September 1942 and Victory in Europe Day 1945 were eventful, at times fearful as when the Luftwaffe raided Eastbourne. During the period that we were at Gonville there were at least 30 air raids. It was judged that during the war the town was subjected to the most air attacks on the south east coast. The conventional air-raid sirens which warned of the approach of enemy planes were controlled on a regional basis. Frequently, raids took place without warning; planes flying low over the sea undetected by radar, flashed up over Beachy Head and descended on the town at 350 mph to drop their bombs. The town's MP, Charles Taylor, and the Town Council made sustained demands to Parliament and the Home Office for a local warning.

Shortly before the Eastbourne Branch was established in Eastbourne, permission was given for a local warning system to be set up. It became known as the cuckoo warning and consisted of the repetition of two notes, said to be similar to the bird's characteristic call. The Royal Observer Corps, made up of experts at aircraft recognition, were principally responsible for triggering the cuckoo warning. When this warning sounded we would rush down into the cellar below Mr Bagnall-Oakeley's quarters. It was arched and brick-lined, distempered in light yellow. It had the appearance of having been a wine cellar in more prosperous days. The raiders were mainly fighter-bombers, the Focke Wulf 190 (FW 190) and the Messerschmitt 109 (ME 109). The former could carry a bomb load of 1,000 kg and the latter 250 kg.

The two most serious incidents, as far as casualties were concerned, were in December 1942 and April 1943. On 18 December 1942, there were two direct hits on Marks & Spencer. There were many shoppers in the store at the time as they had had a delivery of cakes, a scarce commodity in those days. Many were killed and even more were trapped under the debris. A casualty detection team was used to help to locate the trapped victims. On 3 April 1943 there was a direct hit on a surface shelter in Spencer Road, by St Saviour's Church. All those who were sheltering there were killed. Severe damage was sustained in the area around the railway station and Bourne Street, in the east end of town. In the central part of the borough the combined Central Library and Technical Institute was damaged beyond repair. Boys from the branch helped salvage books from the ruins. Next door, in Grove Road, the fire station was also destroyed. Michael Ockenden, a member of the Eastbourne Local History Society, recently researched Luftwaffe records and found that a Focke Wulf 190 had shot up the College tower with its cannons.

Six days after D-Day (the invasion of Europe) many of us were awakened by sounds that were quite different from an ordinary aircraft. We learnt the next day that it was a pilotless plane, the V1, which became known as the doodle-bug. The doodle-bugs were aimed at London and when they reached the target area the engine cut out. This was followed by a menacing silence, except for the sound of it rushing through the air, then a deafening explosion. The majority of boys at Gonville found the doodle-bugs more frightening than raids by conventional planes.

Later in the summer the London-based anti-aircraft units were moved down to the coast with the object of shooting down the doodle-bugs over the sea before they reached a built-up area. The resultant noise took a while to get used to. Later in the summer a V2 (Vengeance Weapon 2) rocket landed with a colossal explosion between Lower Willingdon and Polegate, near Mornings Mill Farm. Fortunately, it landed in open country causing no casualties; the only damage done was a few broken windows. The thought of a continued V2 assault was very disturbing as they struck without warning. They travelled faster than sound, the rushing of their approach being heard after the explosion. Very thankfully, we were told that the rocket had a faulty trajectory and it would be very unlikely that another would land in this area. There was one questionable benefit from German air activity. Candidates taking school or higher school certificate examinations were subject to the invigilators' report on the 'fear factor' caused by concurrent air attacks.

Major operations such as the ill-fated Dieppe raid and the successful D-Day landings were heralded by massive allied air operations. On VE (Victory in Europe) Day the Bagnall-Oakeleys and young boarders celebrated with a picnic on Eastbourne beach, followed by a walk along the foreshore of Beachy Head. A German U-boat surfaced and, as ordered by the Admiralty, the captain endeavoured to offer his surrender to a responsible adult. In this case Bagnall-Oakeley was chosen as the responsible person. However, the situation was resolved when two motor torpedo boats arrived to escort the submarine to Newhaven.

There was a realistic understanding and comradeship between the teaching staff and the boys. In imperceptible ways the staff strengthened our resolve to face up to the uncertainties and dangers of war. We were fortunate in having three excellent masters who provided us with a first-class education. The sacrifices made by staff and their families in leaving the relative safety of Oxfordshire to serve us were much appreciated. In retrospect, many of us have thought what might have been our fate had the Branch not been set up in Eastbourne.

Ted Toovey (Powell 1942) was head boy for much of the time, a task he performed well. He set a good example by being the first cadet to attend an army course. It was a particularly tough one based on physical fitness under war conditions, blank rifle fire and thunder flashes.

The return of the College from Radley for the 1945 Michaelmas term was awaited with a degree of trepidation, which transpired to be quite groundless. George Wilson, the head boy, was endowed with the gift of oratory. He urged us all to do our utmost to re-establish the College's good name now that we were back in Eastbourne. John Nugee, the Headmaster, was a most approachable and caring person. In the afternoon he might be seen pushing his gracious wife in her wheel-chair in Old Wish Road.

For us a new era had begun.

The HMS *Marlborough* Occupation 1942–46

First published in the *Old Eastbournian 2004-5*

by Antonia Beckett with Michael Partridge

Little has been recorded about the fate of the College's buildings in Eastbourne during the war years that followed the evacuation to Radley in 1940. We have been fortunate in tracing two people with first-hand knowledge of that period and shall, so far as possible, let them describe their memories in their own words.

John Cant, a native of Eastbourne, had the good fortune to be posted back to his home town in 1942 as an RAF Armament Instructor. Flying Training Command had established a training school for observers (later navigators), designated No. 1 EAOS (later EANS), with its headquarters in the Sandhurst Hotel on Grand Parade. Personnel were billeted in a number of seafront hotels. 'A' Squadron, as John remembers, occupied the Grand Hotel and used classrooms in the College's Science Building [Design and Technology Building], School House and the Memorial Building. *'It was in the Memorial Block that we Armourers had our workshop where demonstration machine guns, rifles, revolvers, etc. were stored and maintained. Appropriately, we occupied the same store that had been used by the College Cadet Corps. It was interesting to see that the room still retained its nameplate of 'Armoury'. We always found it a most convenient base being on one side of the* [Memorial] *archway leading to the cloisters as, on the other side of the archway, a very popular canteen was set up by a local ladies' organisation.'*

The RAF cannot have continued to use the College premises for very long, for on 24 September 1942 the Royal Navy took occupation, as Miss Antonia Beckett, member of the well-known Eastbourne publishing family, recalls:

'I should like to say that the purpose of the following narrative is to describe the reason for the presence of the Royal Navy in the College buildings during the Second World War and also that of my own association with HMS Marlborough *at that time.*

The Royal Navy came to Eastbourne from their original HQ at HMS Vernon *in Portsmouth, the shore establishment concerned with the uses of underwater weapons.*

HMS Vernon *had been devastated by Nazi bombing and in consequence another 'Vernon' had to be established. As Eastbourne was then a well-known scholastic centre, boasting a great number of schools large and small, it seemed natural, as the children had already been evacuated to safer parts of the country, to use some of the larger ones for the new shore establishment.*

HMS *Marlborough* North Gate

Roedean School near Brighton was also chosen and became HMS Vernon, *while Eastbourne College became HMS* Marlborough [under the command of Captain TG Jackson, RN]. *Both specialised in courses for personnel operating underwater weapons, torpedoes, etc.*

Part of the training consisted of testing weapons actively for which a very large tank was erected in the grounds. [Note: This was located on a part of the site of the Science Centre and was put to secondary use by the Navy as a static water tank and as a swimming-pool. Smaller static water tanks were erected along the north, west and south sides of the College Field. A Naval plan of the *Marlborough* site, undated and slightly illegible, shows the extent to which they colonised not only College properties but other nearby buildings.]

The static water tank

Illustrations were needed to show the various components used in the weapons and it was in this capacity that I became involved. Some of these drawings depicted electrical circuits and others showed the weapon stripped down and 'exploded' to explain the working parts. These charts were strongly constructed and could be at least nine feet in length. The materials were large sheets of cartridge paper backed with canvas and came in large, heavy rolls. Lengths would be cut off according to the size of the work to be done and when finished and approved the whole sheet would be secured top and bottom by long battens. Strong rope attached through the top batten provided a means for hanging the work up for inspection and instruction.

During my student days at the local Art College [this was located in the old library building, the Technical Institute, in Grove Road, destroyed by bombing in February 1943 and rebuilt as the Central Library], *I had never imagined that I would be dealing with machinery but so it transpired. When* Marlborough *had finally been established at the College, steps were taken to recruit artists for the Drawing Office. The Principal of the School of Art was approached to select suitable students for the purpose. I and another girl were thus selected as we had not yet been 'called up' for war service and so it was that we found ourselves working in Eastbourne College where for many years only boys had studied!* [Miss Beckett's starting salary was £2-16s-0d a week.] *My colleague was unable to continue so I was now alone stripping down a lethal bomb (it had been defused). As I discovered more and more about this machine of war, I became fascinated by the precision and colours of the metals, etc., and I found this work to have a certain beauty – after all, I was an artist. It was my job to show how it worked and why. Exploded drawings were the best way to obtain this knowledge.*

It was essential to understand exactly before I could produce a totally correct job and in any case a shoddy one would soon be detected by the man in charge of the Drawing Office [located in the centre of the first floor of the Memorial Building], *Mr Ball, whose keen eyes soon detected any errors.*

All this work was top secret and the security was very strict indeed.

On one occasion I was directed to make sketches of a particular weapon, situated in the driveway of the school opposite the main [School House] *entrance to the College. Prior to the war, this driveway had led to the school* [Clovelly] *where I had been taught to draw from the age of six. It has now been turned into flats. It too had been bombed by the Nazis and people killed. However, the weapon I was directed to was very large and intimidating - a daunting prospect in fact. But as I began to sketch this monster I began to enjoy it, though my mind wandered back to the days when as a pupil I had hastened past the very spot in order to be in school in good time.*

During the war Eastbourne had become a front-line town and was closed to visitors. We had troops almost everywhere and hundreds of people had been evacuated. The population of 50,000 had dropped to 20,000 over one weekend as invasion was expected.

A torpedo tube outside the New Building (now the D&T Building)

We experienced over 100 deliberate raids and one of these will always remain in my memory. It was directed at HMS Marlborough *in particular. A warning had been given over the radio one Friday in April 1943 by 'Lord Haw Haw'*[*]*, the traitor, who promised that the Luftwaffe would pay HMS* Marlborough *a visit. This threat was carried out the next day* [3rd April] *at noon.'*

[Note: 10 or 12 Focke-Wulf 190 fighter-bombers came from the direction of Beachy Head, one of which photographed the 20mm cannon shells striking the College tower. The pilot, a Lieutenant Leopold Wenger, wrote: *'Yesterday, 3rd April, we had to fire on some of the flak positions before we could attack Eastbourne. In the course of the attack, I was hit by flak three times in the wings and fuselage. No doubt these will have been the last shots that gun fired because my cannons did a good job. Our bombs were very effective and shortly after the attack, the whole town was enveloped in smoke and dust.'* HMS *Marlborough* was scarcely damaged, but the Park Gates Hotel in Compton Street, a surface shelter in Spencer Road and other buildings in the town centre were destroyed. The raid resulted in the death in the town of 32 civilians, with injuries to another 99. One of the German aircraft crashed into the sea about 20 miles off Dieppe.]

HMS *Marlborough* Powell Gate

Miss Beckett continues: *We were ordered to the cloisters, which had been heavily protected* [the arches had been bricked up and sandbags stacked in front of the apertures]. *Sited on the top of the College tower* [whose castellations were also bricked up] *were Army gunners* [and a Bofors gun] *who fired at the attackers and caused their bomb*

[*] 'Lord Haw Haw' was born in America of Irish/British parents. His father had taken American citizenship and so William Joyce was an American citizen. In 1933 he obtained a British passport. He had been one of Moseley's British Fascists in the 1930s and was notorious during the war for broadcasting propaganda for the Germans which was intended to undermine British morale. He was executed for treason in 1946, though there was some debate as to whether a non-British national could commit treason. OE Cyril Dalmaine (School House 1918), a journalist working for the *Daily Express,* wrote (under the pseudonym Jonah Barrington) an article in which he gave Joyce the nickname 'Lord Haw Haw', comparing him to one of PG Wodehouse's brainless idiots. The name stuck and did much to make Joyce a figure of fun, rather than a military threat.

loads to be deflected away from the building, to fall on other parts of Eastbourne. Terrible havoc and destruction with many deaths ensued. The College had escaped but an air-raid shelter by St Saviour's Church received a direct hit, killing all the people sheltering there.

Most of the permanent personnel at HMS Marlborough *had seen action at sea when on convoy duties escorting our ships from the USA and many had been wounded or shipwrecked. There were other aspects of the torpedo courses which I really knew nothing about. My colleagues and I just continued to do our particular jobs – drawing the work and inking in the line work, shading the shapes correctly in pencil and cleaning it all ready for the final water-colours which indicated the various parts or electrical circuits. The title and other lettering was also done by hand. Nowadays all this would be achieved in a matter of seconds but then in the 1940s we made these ourselves with pride in our work, glad to feel that we were doing all we could to help those who faced the enemy at sea. We loved our work.*

Rugby v HMS *Marlborough*, 1945

Later we were to see the tanks, Army tanks ready for D Day. They were camouflaged and specially placed under the trees which were in full leaf and even now the resulting uneven brick pavements in parts of Meads can still be seen. They remained there for a while – and all of a sudden they had gone. All these events are a long time ago now but they are still very clear to me – the sense of urgency and the unity of our whole country and especially the words of Mr Churchill. I am very pleased to have been part of a great 'ship' guided safely and expertly by experienced command.

On 24 November 1945 the College 1st XV played against an HMS *Marlborough* team and lost 5–27.

The College's association with HMS *Marlborough* is remembered by the naming of Marlborough House in Old Wish Road, two Mathematics prizes, funded with the surplus moneys accumulated by the Navy's NAAFI Canteen in the Wish, and a stone plaque in the cloisters. In 1992 the 50th anniversary of our association was celebrated by a visit to Eastbourne by the frigate HMS *Marlborough.* Her commanding officer and others of the ship's company attended while the Royal Marines Commando Band beat *Retreat* on College Field.

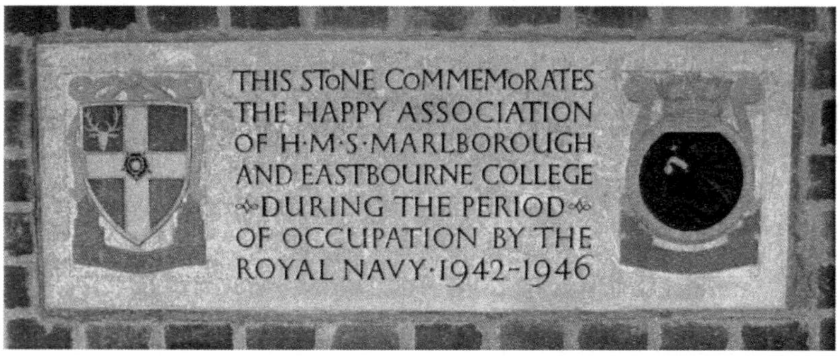

In 1942 the College wisely and in response to a known demand, re-established a presence in Eastbourne, opening a school (Eastbourne College – Eastbourne Branch). It catered for all ages from 8 to 18 in the Gonville building under the leadership of Kem Bagnall-Oakeley, supported by David Craig and Vin Allom. Return from Radley for the remainder of the school was in September 1945, though the Navy remained in possession of School House, the New Buildings, the Masters' Lodge, New Crosby (as Ascham St Vincent's was still called)

and Old Crosby in Blackwater Road well into 1946. So School House was for the moment accommodated in Wargrave with an overflow in Stanhope Court in Silverdale Road. Blackwater, Gonville and Pennell were in their own houses with the day boys in Bendemeer (now Marlborough House) in Old Wish Road. The prep school was housed temporarily in Powell House. The Navy's Nissen huts in the Wish were for a while used by the College as laboratories.

HMS *Marlborough* Spinney Gate

Sources: As well as John Cant and Antonia Beckett, Michael Ockenden has been helpful in finding the naval plan of the HMS *Marlborough* site and also the book *Luftwaffe Fighter-Bombers over Britain* by Chris Goss. This documents, from both sides, the work of Germany's tip-and-run raiders. Euan MacGregor has skillfully restored the naval plan of the HMS *Marlborough* site and Simon Wood has redrawn the *Marlborough* crest.

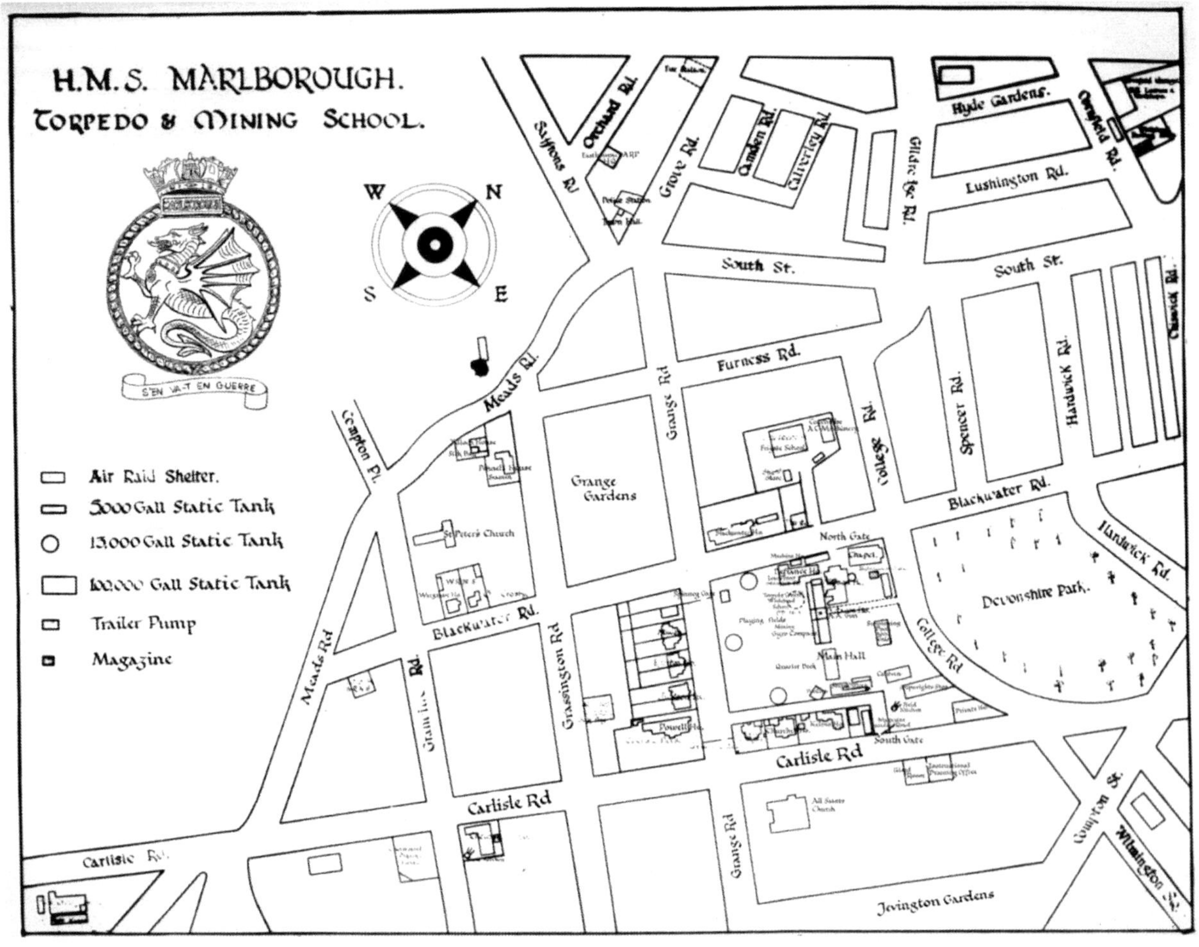